She Prayed

She Loved

She Laughed

Living a Legacy

By Lois 'Lolo' Beshore

World Bible Society
Costa Mesa, CA

She Prayed, She Loved, She Laughed

Copyright 2014 by Lois Beshore

Published by
World Bible Society
PO Box 5000
Costa Mesa, CA 92628

First printing: April 2014

ISBN: 978-1-940241-08-1

Printed in the United States of America

All Scripture quotations are from the American Standard Version.

www.worldbible.org

DEDICATION

This book is dedicated to my incredible husband, who encouraged me to share my story for years, and to my wonderful family, to whom this legacy belongs. I also dedicate this writing to the Lord because in God's Word, I am instructed to encourage *"the young women to love their husbands, to love their children, to be sensible, pure, workers at home, so that the word of God will not be dishonored."* I hope this book will be used as a tool to fulfill God's command to us in Titus 2:4,5 and for you to live your legacy.

To Kenton and our children Mark, Kenette, Kenton, and Kandis

To my Grandchildren: Holiday, Tyler, Buddy, Beau, Cole, Case, Bryce, Trevor, Shanel, Austin, and Taps

To my Great Grandchildren: Kade, Tate, Cosette, Crew, Jack, Miley, Annie, Parker, and Kai

Beshore Family at the wedding of Bryce and Kristen Beshore
Photo Pepper Nix

ACKNOWLEDGMENT

I would like to thank my dear friend, Vickie Sanders, who I have mentored for almost 20 years. Without her investment of hard work and time, this book would not have been possible. I have been encouraged by my husband's wish and her great desire to share my story of service to Jesus Christ along with the insights He gave me with others. Vickie has taken charge of overseeing this endeavor. She brought on Kathy Williamson, who did an excellent job of putting my life story into this book from many recorded interviews and conversations. Glen Megill of ROCK of Africa Mission designed the layout , cover and added photos of many memorable times in my life. I would also like to thank my dear friend of almost 40 years, Dale Sprowl, who invested her time to edit this book. She dedicated a beautiful poem to me, which is included after the last chapter. The Lord has used many others to help that are not mentioned, and I am very grateful to you all.

With Vickie Sanders

CONTENTS

FOREWORD

To meet Lois is a lovely event, to get to know her is a joyful wonder, and to live with her as I have for 67 years is beyond expression. No man, particularly a minister, could have a better wife, companion, and partner, and no kids could have a better mother, grandmother and great grandmother. My life with "Lolo" is a joy. I could not have accomplished nearly as much in my life and ministry without her. She and I have three wonderful children and have had a beautiful life of ministry together. Together we have produced over 15,500 daily radio broadcasts, and we have traveled the world having printed and distributed Bibles in over 100 countries.

Meeting Lois the first time, however, got me off to a rocky start. We were 17 years old, the year was 1943, and we were both registering for college. She was a high school senior in line on one side of a large room, and I was a college freshman in line on the other side of the room. I had been standing in line for forty-five minutes and was fourth from the front when I saw her. She was the most beautiful lady I had ever seen. I, however, had been going with a girl for two years (she later became Miss America). Leaving my line, I went over to meet Lois. I said, "Hi, I'm Kenton Beshore." She said, "I'm Lois Anderson." I said, "I'm from Memphis, Tennessee," and she said, "I'm from Detroit, Michigan." Then while looking into her beautiful blue eyes, I said, "Lois Anderson, I'm going to marry you." She replied, "Kenton, I wouldn't marry you if you were the last man on earth." Then I said, "If I were the last man on earth, you would have to stand in line." Then she turned her back to me, and I had to go back to the end of my line. What a way to start.

I kept asking her for a date. She turned me down eighty-four times. Finally she said, "If I date you, will you promise me never to ask for another date?" I said yes. I lied. I behaved well on that date, and it led to another, eventually leading to marriage two and a half years later.

Our life together has been one of blessing and joy. Lois has given me four children. Our first child died when he was six months old. Then we had Kenette, Kenton, and Kandi. We had a "K" problem. My wife is the most godly person I have ever known. The Bible was on the dining table every evening for reading and prayer after the meal. Sundays after church were great dining and family experiences. Before church Lois started the meal, a beef roast with carrots, onions, mashed potatoes and gravy, and delicious raspberry jello fit for a king. After church we gathered with family and friends around the special table I made with a lazy susan in the middle. These are satisfying memories.

As you read Lois's story, I hope you will not only receive her knowledge and experience, but you will get to encounter Lois herself and learn the legacy she has lived.

— F. Kenton "Doc" Beshore

ONE

Live a Life of Purpose and Intention

Do you know God's purpose for your life? Are you living intentionally or letting life drift by? Proverbs 29:18 states, *"Without a vision, the people perish."* Are you thriving or perishing? In this book, I will help you thrive and become the woman God created you to be and have fun along the way! Through this, you will create a legacy for you and your family.

As I look back on my life, I recognize that what I accomplished was because of my passion to follow God's will. I hope you will receive the knowledge and encouragement to intentionally follow Jesus Christ daily as you see how Biblical principles played out in my life.

In Titus 2:3-5, it says:

> *The older women likewise, that they be reverent in behavior, not slanderers, not given to much wine, teachers of good things — that they admonish the young women to love their husbands, to love their children, to be discreet, chaste, homemakers, good, obedient to their own husbands, that the word of God may not be blasphemed.*

After living for 87 years, I'd like to share what I've learned that has blessed me and helped my family so that you and your family will be blessed, too.

Before I begin to share the thoughts, actions, and attitudes that allowed God to make my life full, I'd like to tell you about my childhood.

Starting at the age of three, my grandmother was a huge influence on me. She loved church and was excited to be there every Sunday. Her feelings were contagious and she put the love of church in my heart too. I am grateful to my God-fearing grandmother. Since my parents were not Christians at the time, she was my first invitation to church. I woke up early and dressed myself and waited eagerly for my grandmother. I wanted to be with my Godly grandmother in the House of the Lord on Sunday. She impressed upon me how fun church was and every Sunday we rode a streetcar across the city. Times have really changed!

I think my folks were glad I was with her at church all day because it gave them a break from me and some much needed time alone. At that time, I was the only young person at the church, and I enjoyed how everyone doted on me. My grandmother remembers that I listened intently to those sermons of old as a young girl attending the main service because there was no Sunday school class. She told me how surprised she was at how good I was as a three year old. "Lois," she said, "You were as good as gold in church today. You never moved a muscle and I am so proud of you." I remember loving to hear the stories about the Bible. I was not yet a

Christian, but I can't remember a time when I didn't have a strong urge to hear and learn about the Lord.

As the church grew, they added a Sunday school class. I was thrilled. One Sunday soon after I entered the Sunday school classroom, (a simple curtained off area in a very small church) my teacher asked if I had ever accepted Jesus as my savior. When I said no, she was surprised because I had never missed a Sunday. I had always felt the presence of the Lord, and that He was with me and watching over me. But that Sunday, after I had accepted the Lord as my Savior, God immediately put love in my heart for Him and a strong desire to be used of Him and to do His will.

That day I remember that my Sunday school teacher walked by each student's chair to pray out loud over each of us. I wanted to hear what she would pray over me. When she reached my chair, I sat still as she prayed, "Dearest Jesus, I believe Lois has great love and a great ability to serve You. Would You, please Father, bless this future leader and use her for Your glory?" I remember her saying that just for me and I thought to myself...*Hmmm, if she thinks I am a leader, I must be. I wonder what God has planned for me?* She prayed and spoke that beautiful prayer into my life.

To all Sunday school teachers working to create lessons for their students, I want to say, I will never forget the kindness and love of that wonderful woman. I remember her as if it were yesterday and I thank God for her willingness to put God's stories and love into my heart and mind. I am forever grateful that she volunteered to be my Sunday school teacher, that she was brave enough to ask me the question even though I had never missed a Sunday, and that she lead me to the Lord at the age of nine.

Soon my parents also became Christians. I had begged them to come to church with Grandma and me, so they finally came. After three Sundays, they went forward to ask Jesus into their hearts. Like daughter, like parents in this case. My mother always had the gift of hospitality, so after they became Christians, my parents' home was open for every Bible study and youth meeting for the whole church.

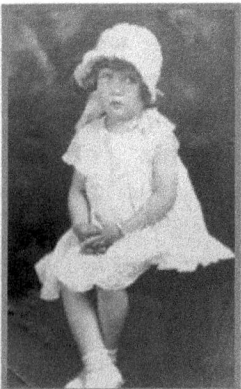

My father was a very bright man even though he had never graduated from elementary school. He had to drop out in the fifth grade to work to support his family. My mother only attended school through tenth grade. My father and his brother, my uncle Willis, were scrappy emigrants from Sweden who began to make steel parts for the government. By the time World War I started, they had a lucrative business making parts for tanks for the war. Those two brothers together had the ability to make money and they did.

My parents had a large home, and they used it for the Lord. The pastor came over and they prayed that God would be glorified in their home. My parents modeled how to use anything that God gave them for Him. I admired my mother greatly because she walked the walk and talked the talk better than anyone else I have known.

Before I graduated from high school, we held many youth meetings in our home, but many of my friends chose to go in different directions. They went to colleges, had a grand time, and joined sororities. When I visited them at college, they introduced me to their sororities. I realized I did not want to participate in what they were doing. I didn't want to judge them, but to me, it was a waste of time. Even in those days, sororities were wild so I told my parents I decided to go away to a Christian school. I was a senior in high school and my folks had the money to send me to a Christian college. I planned to go to Wheaton Academy.

However when my family went to a Maranatha Bible Conference and I heard Dr. Bob Jones preach, I knew I was headed in a different direction. He suggested that I come to his school, Bob Jones University. Instantly I knew the Lord was leading me there. That Sunday, the president of Wheaton called and said, "We would love to have you come to our school," but I felt God wanted me to go to Bob Jones University instead. When I arrived at the university, I realized there was a special reason why God had sent me there. It was to meet my husband.

In the forward of this book, you heard the story of how I met Kenton in the registration line at Bob Jones. Two years after we met, we were engaged to be married. I knew he was the one when I watched him preach. I was excited to be a pastor's wife.

Doc and I have been married for over 67 years. We have four beautiful children. Mark was our first child, however, he went home to heaven when he was six months old. The Lord then blessed us with three more beautiful children: Kenette, Kenton, and Kandis. We currently have ten grandchildren and nine great-grandchildren. You will learn more about some of them as you read this book.

Throughout my life, it has been my desire to follow God's leading. My passion eventually developed into becoming a Proverbs 31 woman—not just talking the talk, but walking the walk. That meant my being in the Word and in prayer regularly.

Another passion throughout my life has been to pray for God's wisdom and to encourage those around me to do the same. If you ask my grandchildren or great-grandchildren, they'll tell you that I ask them all the time, "Have you prayed for wisdom today?" I do this daily and sometimes even hourly. Whenever someone calls and asks a question, I pray, "God, give me the wisdom to answer in a godly manner and to use Your Word not just my words."

In order for me to be in God's Word, I have to be intentional. That's why my life verse is Proverbs 3:5-6:

*Trust in the LORD with all your heart; and lean not on
your own understanding; In all your ways
acknowledge Him, and He shall direct your paths.*

I quote this verse to myself all the time. I've prayed for many things, sometimes for as long as five years, which God has not yet seen fit to answer. I choose to trust in the Lord with all my heart. I'm not going to lean on my own understanding just because I don't like the way it's turning out. But in all my ways, I'm going to acknowledge that the Lord is the Lord, and I'm not, and He will direct my path. That is the verse I bank on: I trust in Him, and that He is going to lead my life and show me what to do.

In today's fast-paced, self-centered society, it takes being deliberate if you want to be a Godly woman who trusts the Lord in all situations. Developing the right habits and attitudes will help you grow into being that person. Have I always succeeded in doing everything right? Oh no. I've made many mistakes, and I've had lots of do-overs in my life, but I have always thought sincerely in my heart to *trust in the Lord*. I wanted to do what was right even though I didn't do it all of the time. Whenever I thought about living life my way and not His way, it scared me. I did not say, "I'm going to do this, Lord, whether You want me to or not," rather, "Lord, I want to serve You. Show me what You want me to do." I had seen others do their own thing and seen the results of that behavior, and I didn't want that.

Because I have looked to God for His strength, guidance, and wisdom throughout my life, He has enabled me to run a mortuary, to teach in seminary, to speak in many places, to help my husband with our ministry daily at the World Bible Society, and do many other things for Him. I encourage women of all ages to pray for wisdom daily. This allows you to be the Godly working person or wife and mother that God wants you to be. It keeps you from going beyond your own abilities and helps you become the person that you should be at home.

If you're young, you may not be thinking right now about what type of legacy you want to leave. When I was busy with three growing children, I didn't think about what my legacy would be. But now is the time to be purposeful with your life. Now is the time to ask yourself what type of legacy you want to leave. I hope my children will say I was a Godly woman at home, that I did what God wanted me to do, and that I was there for them day in and day out. On a one-to-one basis, I can look each of my family members in the eye and tell them, "I did the best I could for you." I want to be able to say I was the best mother that I could be, I was the best grandmother I could be, I was the best great-grandmother I could be, and I was the best wife I could be.

That is why I want to share my story. When I first went into the ministry, there were no books to help Christian women in ministry or give them guidance. I had only one thing to rely on, *"But if any of you lacks wisdom, let him ask of God, who gives to all liberally and without reproach, and it will be given to him."* –James 1:5

I remember one time when I needed that wisdom. We had a large church in Minneapolis, and I was invited to attend a ministers' wives meeting. I thought I needed to go because I wanted to learn how to be a good minister's wife, and I didn't have anybody to help me. So I went and all I heard was griping and complaining. I was shocked. As I left to go home, they said , "We hope you'll be back, Lois." I said, "No, I won't be back." They asked, "Why not?" I said, "All you've done is complain and gripe about serving the Lord, and I don't want to be like that. I came here to learn how I could serve the Lord more effectively and how I could be a better wife and a better minister's wife, but I didn't learn that today." They were all slack-jawed as I left that ministers' wives' gripe session. I never returned. It is important to work hard daily to be positive and grateful and to be what God wants us to be.

Life Principle: To Be a Godly Woman,
Live Life Intentionally

If you've never thought about living an intentional life, here are some practical guidelines to help you begin.

To live intentionally, you have to know how God wants you to live. To be a Godly woman, you need to know and believe that you need Him every moment. This awareness is our greatest strength. Throughout the Bible, there are general guidelines for living, as well as unique and personal guidance for your life. It is important to begin to recognize each of these. Make God the central theme in your consciousness by praying continually. Even if they are short prayers, keep on asking Him, and you will receive. Say His name all day long. Call out "God, help me!" or "Help me, Jesus!" When you call out in His name, He will hear you! 1 Thessalonians 5:17 says, *"Pray without ceasing,"* and John 16:24 instructs us: *"Until now you have asked nothing in My name. Ask, and you will receive, that your joy may be full."*

Once you start following this idea of keeping God the central theme in your life, you will receive God's guidance. If you happen to go down the wrong path, God will show you. If you're communicating with Him through prayer, reading the Word, and talking to Him because He is there all day long, then the Spirit will show you what to do and how to get back on the right path when you wander off.

Sometimes we get so excited about something we want to do that we forget to include the Lord in it. Has this ever happened to you? James 4:15 reminds us that *"Instead you ought to say, "If the Lord wills, we shall live and do this or that."* Another principle for finding God's will is to listen to those around you who love you, like your husband and good friends. When I ask them, I want them to honestly hold me accountable not to shell out sunshine. I want them to be the iron that sharpens me, even if it hurts.

My life intention is to do what the Lord wants me to do and to give Him all the glory. Based upon this priority, I make Him central in my consciousness and I pray continually. If I wanted to do something selfish, God would convict me. I always pray short but weighty prayers, like "Lord, be with me," and He listens and helps me to put others ahead of myself.

My priorities are: the Lord, my husband, my children, grandchildren, great-grandchildren, and then ministry. By working hard to keep this proper perspective, the Lord has blessed me in each area of my life, and He will also bless you.

Ecclesiastes 12:13-14 sums up the goal of life:

> *Fear God, and keep His commandments, for this is man's all. For God will bring every work into judgment, including every secret thing, whether good or evil.*

❖ What is your life goal?

❖ How are you living life intentionally?

❖ What are the areas in your life where you need to make corrections in order to be in line with God's Word?

> *If any of you lacks wisdom, let him ask of God, who gives to all liberally and without reproach, and it will be given to him. But let him ask in faith, with no doubting, for he who doubts is like a wave of the sea driven and tossed by the wind. For let not that man suppose that he will receive anything from the Lord; he is a double-minded man, unstable in all his ways.*
> —James 1:5-8

TWO
2

Build Character
God's Way

haracter is revealed by our actions. *"Even a child is known by his deeds, whether what he does is pure and right"* (Proverbs 20:11). We cannot hide from God nor from man. While the characteristic tendencies of each generation are different, God's view of godly character is the same.

One of my lifelong prayers has been, "Be on guard against the pit of self-pity." My trap was when I got weary. To protect myself from self-pity, I occupied my mind with praising and thanking Him. If you do this, it is impossible to fall into the pit. The closer you stay to Him, the farther you stay away from that pit.

Some of the character traits of my generation—don't forget I'm 87 years old at this time—are different from today's. One trait I had going for me is that I put my family before myself. My generation was not the "me" generation. It was the "others" generation. Many women did not take good care of themselves back then. Today I think it is a fine line between being able to take care yourself, to love yourself, and also to ask, "What would be best for my family and for my children?" Today there is much stress to look fabulous, to work out, and to have a job. It is important to take care of yourself and I did not do that enough. Instead, I invested in my family's lives. I invested in their interests and activities consistently.

It's not easy for some women to lay aside the strong motivation to do everything their own way and in their own timing. It's hard to place our own desires before the Lord and choose to follow Him. Only by prayer and practice and knowing the Word of God can we shift our priorities. We need to be ever cognizant that we are prone to be selfish. I was a spoiled child, but I learned when I got married that if I was going to have the marriage God wanted me to have, I had to learn to give and give to others, and take and take from the Lord. I had to learn that with my kids, and I had to learn that with my grandkids.

We need to recognize our propensity to be selfish, and that to overcome it, we need to be in the Word daily. By being in His Word and keeping our eyes on Him, we trust Him more and more. This choice must be made every day. The more we choose to trust Him, the easier it becomes.

Whenever somebody calls and says, "I want advice," I say, "I don't give advice any more." (Thank God, I realized that I am not a good god.) I don't try to live someone else's life for them. I try to be the person that God wants me to be. When I'm being the person God wants me to be, I will be able to bless others. I will not always be thinking of myself or what is best for me. If I read the Word of God, I will be in a place where God wants me to be.

Being in the Word is a real problem for me right now because my eyesight is bad. I have to use a magnifying glass, and I have to use an extra light on everything. I have macular degeneration, the kind that cannot be cured. This diagnosis is a challenge for me, and I have to deal with not being able to see very well. But I'm not going to let this stop me from being in the Word. I am listening to the Word daily in audio format. I have memorized Scriptures throughout my life, and as I get older, I need to quote those Scriptures to remind myself to practice them: *"Your word I have hidden in my heart, that I might not sin against You."* –Psalm 119:11

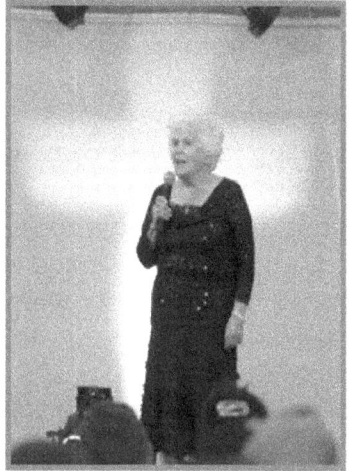

Every night before I go to bed, I ask myself, "In the light of eternity, what have I done for the Lord today?" One of my morning prayers is, "Thank you, Lord, for health, strength, and the privilege of serving You. What do You want me to do today?" Is it always easy? No! But I do it because I want to please my Lord.

Part of the problem with being self-centered is that it can lead to being prideful. In today's society, self-centeredness is promoted. Unfortunately, this leads to problems. When I am prideful and selfish, I am trying to become a god. Only God is a good God!

The Bible tells us not to think too highly about ourselves:

> *For I say, through the grace given to me, to everyone who is among you, not to think of himself more highly than he ought to think, but to think soberly, as God has dealt to each one a measure of faith.* –Romans 12:3

This dying to selfishness permeates every area of our lives. It illustrates our motives. Are we living to serve the Lord and do what He wants us to do, or are we turning away from God and determining to do things our way, no matter what? Submitting to God is NOT an easy assignment. Our desire to live under the Lord and in His presence goes against the grain of the world, the flesh, and the devil. Much of our weariness results from our constant battle against these opponents of living under the Lord and dying to ourselves. God has said in Romans and in Ephesians that He is above all things, all of our problems, all of our pain, and all of the events in our ever-changing world. When we behold His face, we can rise above ourselves and our circumstances and rest in Him in heavenly realms. This is peace.

Whenever you feel yourself sinking into the sea of circumstances and wanting to go your own way, say out loud, "Help me, Jesus, to look to You," and He will draw you back to Him. I had to say this many times a day. He says to us, "Don't be discouraged, you will always have problems and pride in this life." He knows our weaknesses, and He will meet us in our weak places, even when we want to be self-centered.

When you do what the Lord tells you to do, He blesses you in many ways beyond what you could ever achieve on your own. Do I have any regrets for living this way? No! The blessings far outweigh any sacrifices. We can never outgive God!

Life Principle: Die to Self-Centeredness and Receive God's Blessings

---

A life focused on serving God and others always trumps a life of being self-centered. If you look to God, He will help you change.

❖ In what ways are you being self-centered?

❖ How can you turn that around to focus on loving and serving others?

❖ If you're married, talk with your husband and ask him in what ways you can love and serve him better.

Let no one seek his own, but each one the other's well-being. – I Corinthians 10:24

Godliness and integrity go hand in hand. Godliness shows us the right path to take in life and integrity helps us to stay on it. "*Let integrity and uprightness preserve me, for I wait for You*" (Psalm 25:21). Living a life of integrity will keep us out of many problems.

Speaking at Sanctuary Church in Calimesa, California

Integrity is who we are inside. It is making sure that we do what is right in all parts of our lives and in all the things we tell our children to do. One time I remember I was at the store and the clerk gave me back too much money. My daughter was with me as I said to the clerk, "I'm sorry, I think that five dollars is yours." Kenette looked at me as I gave it back to her. She said, "Mom, she gave it to you." I told her, "That isn't mine." Integrity is showing your children that we practice what we try to teach them to do.

Being a person of integrity goes along with not being self-centered. Sometimes when a person is self-centered, he or she will compromise the Word in order to get ahead. A person can become more focused on achievement rather than doing what's right.

Integrity means having a true heart and following it. This is especially important for leaders in ministry. No matter how much charisma and natural leadership ability someone has, he or she must also have a genuine heart and be willing to follow God's instructions.

Integrity means we must walk what we talk and it shows that we are spiritually mature. If we want a reputation that is pleasing to the Lord, then we must BE that person. When you blow it, apologize to God, to others, and then move on. Don't look back, stay stuck, or pretend it didn't happen. Be proactive asking God to reveal what He wants you to do. No one is perfect, but by taking action, you are being a responsible person of integrity. This means trusting what God says is true, even if we can't see His perspective on the situation at the moment.

15

❖ In what areas of your life are you talking one way, but acting another?

❖ How can you rectify that situation today?

❖ In your life goals, what areas might you be tempted to compromise and stray from God's path?

❖ Will you commit today to not compromise in any area of your life and to seek God's wisdom and guidance and follow them? When you do blow it, ask God for light on the situation. When He convicts you, ask Him to forgive you. If you need to ask forgiveness of someone you might have caused to stumble, do it. Let your heart be soft to the Lord and trust Him. He does His greatest work through people with trusting and soft hearts towards Him.

Your word is a lamp to my feet and a light to my path.
–Psalm 119:105

If we confess our sins, He is faithful and just to forgive us our sins and cleanes us from all unrighteousness. – I John 1:9

THREE

Pursue Daily
Spiritual Growth

f we're not growing spiritually, we're slipping backwards. There is no neutral ground. We must pursue spiritual growth in our lives. Sometimes we can get so caught up in the day-to-day demands that our time spent reading the Word and being with God seems to disappear. Pretty soon, it's been a whole week and we haven't even talked to God.

Life Principle: Be In the Word Daily

The most important spiritual principle is to read the Word daily. My passion is to start each day with the Word. Since I'm a morning person, it's easier for me than it is for others.

Before my feet ever hit the floor, I ask for wisdom. Then I thank the Lord, praising Him for health and strength and the privilege of serving Him. It has been a little harder lately because of my eyesight and my bionic knee and shoulder. But then I realize I am blessed because I have had good eyesight, knees, and shoulders for 84 years. I have had many great years on the tennis courts. With only three bad years out of 87, I have a lot of praising to do.

We need gratitude. Many times we are not grateful for what we do have, and we're anxious for things that we do not have. Praise and thanksgiving have guided my life along with the Word of God. Rejoice and be thankful. As you walk with Him throughout the day, practice trusting and thanking Him along the way. It lifts you up, above and out of your day-to-day circumstances. It gives you altitude and the ability to see your life as He sees it.

We also have to be deliberate in showing our children how important being in the Word daily will be in their lives. We keep the Bible on the table as a regular reminder that we need to look to it for answers. This is much easier to do when the children are smaller than when they get older. If you start this when they are young, it becomes a habit as the years go by.

I have spoken to many mothers of teenagers, and they have begun to read the Word of God after dinner to their teenagers. Even if they walk away from the table, which has happened several times, the moms kept on reading their daily devotional out loud. The children of most of these women and men finally realize the importance of this daily form of inspiration. One of the teenagers of a good friend of mine began reading it herself, and when her parents forgot, she said, "Sit down. We haven't read our Scripture yet!"

When our children were younger, we had a devotion time each night. This also included an exercise where each of us shared "the peak" and "the pit" of the day. You could have two peaks, but you couldn't have two pits. Many times we learned the difficult things that went on in school with our children. Maybe somebody had hurt their feelings or something happened at school that was a pit for them. We said, "Oh, we are so sorry about that. What can we do?

Do you want us to go to school and make that right?" We let them know that we cared. Many times we found out about things that we would never have learned without this exercise. We could then pray about that situation later on, or we could pray together right then.

Life Principle: Don't Major on the Minors

Because my husband was a pastor, we didn't have a lot of money. We lived in an affluent area in La Canada, and our children saw many people getting a lot of things and relying on these material goods for their happiness. I had to remind my children when their friends got brand new cars, *"And my God shall supply all your needs according to His riches in glory by Christ Jesus"* (Philippians 4:19). It was hard at times to get this across because when we said, "These are just things and they don't bring happiness," I remember my children would say, "My friends look pretty happy to me about their new car!"

Many times we try to fill the empty void inside us with material possessions. People, even Christians, end up buying more and more, and never become fully satisfied. Throughout my life, I've found that if I feed upon the Word regularly, my soul gets fed, and I'm satisfied. It says in Matthew 4:4, "But He answered and said, *"It is written, 'Man shall not live by bread alone, but by every word that proceeds from the mouth of God.'"*

The Word is the only book that is alive. The Holy Spirit speaks to us through the Word and also through our prayers. Without reading the Word or praying, our soul's longings will not be satisfied.Not only does our relationship with God fill us, but He also wants to show us how to live each day. He wants to show us that our life has meaning beyond the daily grind. Our first purpose is to love God and then to love others. However, to find out how God wants us to act in certain situations, we have to be in the Word daily.

He waits patiently for us to come close and talk to Him. He longs to speak with us, to fellowship with us, and to see our faces turned toward Him in worship every day. Jesus tells us to seek His face. A verse that has been a blessing to me is Psalm 105:4, "*Seek the LORD and His strength; Seek His face evermore!*"

This is not an easy road to be on, this journey of intimacy with Him. If we could realize that God is our treasure, and we should be on the hunt for Him, then we would do whatever it takes to find the time to spend with God. I'm not saying we need to neglect our duties as women, wives and mothers, but in order to be the women God wants us to be, we have to spend time with Him. There are no other substitutes.

Life Principle: Daily Bible Reading Keeps You Growing

I never tire of reading the Bible. Since it is *alive*, I can read and reread the same passage over and over and get a new and different message from it each time. If I don't spend time in the Word, it is similar to not spending any time with my husband, Doc. Our relationship would never grow. After a while, if we never talked to each other, we would drift apart. The same is true of our relationship with God. If we don't spend time talking to God and also listening to Him talk to us, our relationship won't grow. It's not something that I "have" to do—it's something I "get" to do. I get to talk to the almighty God, and He hears me. What's even better is that He talks to me, and He even answers my prayers!

❖ Are you reading and meditating upon the Word daily? If not, will you commit to do so, starting today? What are some of the barriers you must overcome to find this time each day to read the Bible?

❖ If you don't know where to start or how to keep yourself reading it every day, pick up a good topical Bible study to get you started. Choose a topic in an area where you're either struggling or you want to grow more. Then keep repeating this process.

❖ How about my "peaks and pits" exercise? Can you add

that to your daily evening Bible reading with your children? Or can you and your spouse add this as you review your day's activities?

Be diligent to present yourself approved to God, a worker who does not need to be ashamed, rightly dividing the word of truth. – II Timothy 2:15

Make the Word Applicable

Another way to enhance your Bible reading is to find ways to make it applicable every day. Throughout my life I have looked for specific examples from my work or ministry to share with my children of how to apply Biblical principles to those situations. Since I taught in seminary and ran a mortuary, I was able to bring some of those experiences home.

For instance, during the time I was working at the mortuary, one evening during our family devotions, I said, "You know the thing I heard today from the loved ones of the deceased was... 'I wish I had said.. .'" Often we neglect to express how important the people that we love the most are to us while they're still alive. I heard that many times as I ran the mortuary. It was "I wish I had said. . . " or "I wish I had told him. . . ." I continually express how I feel about each member of our family. I want to tell them now, not to wait until later or I am no longer here. I affirm them now with warm hands. I do not want to die without having said the words I mean.

Since I heard this repeatedly at the mortuary, I began to express love and affirm my children more and more. I began to tell them how I appreciated the actions and attributes I saw in them. I told them how brave they were. I remember telling my son, Kenton, how proud I was of him because as a young high school kid, he ran our whole worship service every single Sunday. (I still tell him what great messages he gives and what a wonderful visionary he is!) I told our youngest, Kandi, how proud I was that she was such a good friend to her friends and how hospitable she was. She was always inviting others to come home with her, and she never left anyone out. She is still like that today, and I tell her that often. I told Kenette how much I loved her heart of mercy and that I appreciated what a great leader she was, and I am still telling her that all of the time today.

Back in the 1970s when my kids were growing up, there was a horrible push for kids to take drugs. During that time, *McCalls* magazine published an article that stated there was nothing wrong with marijuana, that it was safe to use. In *Psychology Today,* there was another article stating they could find nothing harmful or addicting about cocaine, and that it was good to take for wakefulness! The 70's were called the sexual revolution and society was crazy back then. Parents didn't have educated help on how to deal with the decisions their kids were making. I consider myself fortunate that my kids never did drugs, that they chose to be leaders, and that they chose to remain abstinent. They made decisions with their values in mind and they kept their promises and the contracts they had made with us about how they were going to live and how they were going to be a light to their friends at school.

I don't mean to brag, but my kids were (especially now that I look back and hear the horror stories of today) very easy to raise.

I can remember my friends always saying, "Lois, your kids are going to have big heads. You need to keep them humble. You are way too generous with praising them." I disagreed with my friends because I saw firsthand the heartbreak of loved ones who had never expressed how they felt. They were afraid or they never took the time to look for great character traits in their children and loved ones.

Whenever I affirmed my children for these inward qualities of character, I saw them light up like flashbulbs. Those affirmations produced self-respect and self-esteem. God was working with them and for them, and I tried to make that clear to them. I wanted them to see themselves and their circumstances from God's perspective. I wanted to give them perspective so that they could see their blessings from the Lord. Then I watched as God helped them be better followers and students and lovers of Him.

When you affirm your children, be honest and point out specific qualities of character. Pour it on, but be truthful because dishonesty will make your child insecure. If you're affirming your children for their outside appearance or about traits that they know are not true, they will know and your praises will be empty. Then your words won't be sweet, but bitter. You can't kid a kid.

Today's parents have an opportunity to impact their children if they will only learn to be vulnerable and allow their children to see how they themselves apply the Word to their situation. Parents can even have a discussion time where they share what's going on in their lives (using discretion of course, based upon the circumstances and the ages of the children) and how they're applying the Word to their situation or how they're praying and trusting God to guide them.

In order for this to occur, the family needs to slow down long enough to come together as a family—perhaps around the dinner table each night—to allow these times of sharing to happen. In many families, the father works late. I encourage mothers to use this opportunity to interact with your children. Sometimes we can't wait until everything is perfect (like if the father is not there at the moment we want to go for a family walk or play a game). We must seize every opportunity, every day, to be the godly woman and mother God wants us to be.

My husband and I seized time together when we were driving. The other day I saw a mom driving her kids around with a movie on in the back and the teenager in front on her cell phone. I am blessed that I didn't have to deal with the technology of today which so easily sidetracks children. Our drive times were our sacred times to instill what God was teaching us, to affirm our children, or to ask them what God was teaching them in their lives.

The best way to teach our children how to live the Christian life is to show them every day how practical it is. Every night, (except for Friday night which was our date night and Saturday night which was pizza night), we read the Word of God together with our children. It wasn't a long and involved event. The Bible was on the table, and we read and prayed with them. This was how we helped make God's Word practical in their lives. They saw how we integrated it into our daily lives. Was it always fun? No. Was it a chore sometimes? Yes, but we kept it up as a regular practice. As a mother, it makes a difference when to maintain the disciplines that are right, whether they are easy or not.

Life Principle: The Word Becomes Practical When
You Understand Real Life Applications

Learning how to apply biblical principles to our lives is not something we learn just once. There is no formula to follow because our circumstances and spiritual maturity are different each time we approach the Word looking for guidance. Will you always find your specific situation in the Word? No. What you will find are stories of people who had to deal with similar temptations, decisions, emotional turmoil, unanswered questions, various types of wrong thinking, and consequences of actions which contradicted God's instructions. When you look for answers, you will be encouraged to make wise choices because you will read about God's faithfulness to love and provide for His people.

To apply God's Word in our lives requires an attitude of humility. It's easy to think that because "my" solution worked last time, that it will work in my current situation. Unfortunately, sometimes we have to learn the hard way. Then, when it doesn't work out, we turn to the Word to find a solution. It would be much easier if we applied God's principles first, then we could avoid the problem in the first place.

Here are some questions to prompt your thinking about how you can share with family and friends how to apply the Word to your life.

❖   Are you going to the Word first to find out how to handle a situation? If so, what are some of the keywords you use to find guidance for your life?

❖ Looking at your past, what situations did you try to handle on your own, and then when you failed, you turned to God for guidance?

❖ What's going on in your life right now that you need to ask God for His guidance? What keywords can you use to find direction from the Word?

The law of the LORD is perfect, converting the soul: the testimony of the LORD is sure, making wise the simple. The statutes of the LORD are right, rejoicing the heart: the commandment of the LORD is pure, enlightening the eyes. The fear of the LORD is clean, enduring for ever: the judgments of the LORD are true and righteous altogether. More to be desired are they than gold, yea, than much fine gold: sweeter also than honey and the honeycomb. Moreover by them is thy servant warned: and in keeping of them there is great reward. – Psalm 19:7-11

Prayer

I have been a devout and consistent person of prayer all of my life. It has impacted my life and the lives of those for whom I have prayed. As our kids were growing up, and even today, I asked them, "How can I pray for you today?" They always knew mom was praying for them, and I think that gave them comfort. But more importantly, it made the greatest impact when they saw God answer their specific prayer requests.

Whenever anyone calls me on the phone, I ask God to give me His words to say. Prayer isn't confined to a specific time we set aside every day. Prayer is something that happens throughout the day, sometimes even moment by moment.

Every morning I go on my walk around several blocks in the neighborhood. Each of my children had a designated block where I pray just for that one as I walk the block. My children know that mom is always praying for them in the mornings. In fact, my daughter, Kenette, wrote a small booklet describing my daily prayers for the children and grandchildren. It has been reprinted in Appendix A to give you an idea of the impact praying for your children can have.

I've also had to pray over and over for certain situations throughout my life. Did God always answer right away? Not always. God's timing on when He answers my prayers is different from when I want the answer to come. We have all had God answer in the eleventh hour, just when we were about to give up on Him responding. Unfortunately, we don't always know when that eleventh hour is. We want our answers right now, like microwave Christianity. We want to be changed instantly, and we want everything to be right instantly. I am always in a hurry, but God never is.

I have found God to be faithful. My part is to maintain my faith that He will answer as His Word tells me. When I lay my burden on the Lord, then God gives me a peace which I can't attain on my own.

Be anxious for nothing, but in everything by prayer and supplication, with thanksgiving, let your requests be made known to God; and the peace of God, which surpasses all understanding, will guard your hearts and minds through Christ Jesus. – Philippians 4:6-7

Sometimes we think that if we keep praying hard enough and long enough that God will eventually hear us and respond. But that's not how God works. When we pray, believing that God hears us and has answered us, then we can stand in faith until the answer is shown. Is it easy? No. Because when the answer doesn't come quickly enough, we think we need to re-pray and petition God again. But instead we need to start thanking God and praising Him for the answer He has already given. This praise and thanksgiving keeps us at peace, as well as moves God to perform His part. We can't manipulate God. Do you remember in the Old Testament in 2 Chronicles 20 where God told the armies to put the singers in the front of the procession going into battle? Why? Because they had their priorities right—it was God who fought their battles for them. And He did. In fact, in that story in Scripture, the people of God did not have to enter into the physical fight. God caused their enemies to turn upon themselves and they killed each other.

The prayer in 2 Chronicles 20:6-12 shows how Jehoshaphat reminded God of who He is and what His promises are. We may think, *God knows who He is, why should we remind Him?* But God tells us to put Him in remembrance. Isaiah 43:26 shows us this, "*Put Me in remembrance: let us contend together: state your case, that you may be acquitted.*"

While we wait for answers to our prayers, we can remember God and His promises to us. This builds our faith and calms us as we review God's faithfulness.

Prayer must be based upon God's Word, not on my own list of desires. The Bible is God's manual for how we are to live. As we search the Word for answers to our problems, sometimes we'll find things that we need to do first before God will perform on His promise. That's when we can pray and ask God to help us change our attitude and/or our actions to line up with His Word. In fact, we should be praying His Word back to Him. We are assured that His Word will not return to Him in an empty way. Isaiah 55:11: "*So shall My word be that goes forth out of My mouth; it shall not return to Me void, but it shall accomplish what I please, and it shall prosper in the thing for which I sent it.*"

Be careful not to pray about something God stated haqs stated in the Bible we should do. That's why I spend so much time in the Word. I've got to know what God wants me to do every day. Sometimes I'll be praying for someone who is doing something wrong according to the Bible. Then I ask God to show that person what they're doing wrong. It's not up to me to change that person. We can't change other people, but God can.

Just remember, God acts beyond our comprehension. We should always expect Him to answer our prayers and to answer them in His way.

Life Principle: Prayer Changes You
and Your Circumstances

Prayer moves the hand of God when we pray according to His will. God has given man a free will and He will not force Himself into our situations. Are there times when God moves miraculously without us even asking? Certainly. We cannot control God in the same way that God does not control all of our actions. I can only work on me and do my part in living out what I see in the Word, praying to God for His assistance, and praising Him every day for His faithfulness to me.

❖ What promises of God are you believing in your prayers? Are there conditions you must fix first before God can respond? What are they and when will you make the necessary changes?

❖ How can you rearrange your schedule so you have a time and place each day to spend reading the Word and praying?

❖ In what areas can you start believing God for big answers? Are you preparing yourself now so that you're ready when those answers come? Are you ready for doors to open and divine appointments to come your way?

❖ Do you need to change your "barely get by" attitude into one of "God will provide abundantly in my life and in my situation?"

The Apostle Paul gave us a great prayer example that we can all use for ourselves as well as others:

Therefore I also, after I heard of your faith in the Lord Jesus and your love for all the saints, do not cease to give thanks for you, making mention of you in my prayers: that the God of our Lord Jesus Christ, the Father of glory, may give to you the spirit of wisdom and revelation in the knowledge of Him, the eyes of your understanding being enlightened; that you may know what is the hope of His calling, what are the riches of the glory of His inheritance in the saints, and what is the exceeding greatness of His power toward us who believe, according to the working of His mighty power which He worked in Christ when He raised Him from the dead and seated Him at His right hand in the heavenly places. – Ephesians 1:15-20*

Legalism versus Grace

Legalism means different things, depending upon what time period you are considering. The word "legalism" does not occur in the Bible. It is a term used to describe a set of rules and regulations a person must follow in order to obtain a reward. Some non-Christian churches use it as part of the salvation process. But Galatians 2:16 shows us where this is wrong: *"Knowing that a man is not justified by the works of the law, but by faith in Jesus Christ, even we have believed in Christ Jesus, that we might be justified by faith in Christ, and not by the works of the law: for by the works of the law no flesh shall be justified."*

In the same way that the people in the Old Testament added their own set of interpretations to what the law meant; many today add their own set of rules and regulations that must be followed in order to be spiritual.

Legalism means rules and regulations a person follows that are not based on God's Word. Legalism is based upon whether **you** think something is right or wrong rather than what God's Word says is right or wrong. It's setting up a false standard of behavior and thinking that it is God's standard. Basically you are becoming a god, a god of the rules of how you should or shouldn't live.

Grace is receiving that which we don't deserve. Grace isn't something that is given out in measure. It's not something that grows, but we can grow in our understanding of grace. Jesus allows us to live under grace instead of under the law. We can grow in our appreciation of the grace we have been given. The more we learn about Jesus, the more we will appreciate all He has done. The more we appreciate His love and sacrifice for us, the more we will perceive the never-ending grace of God.

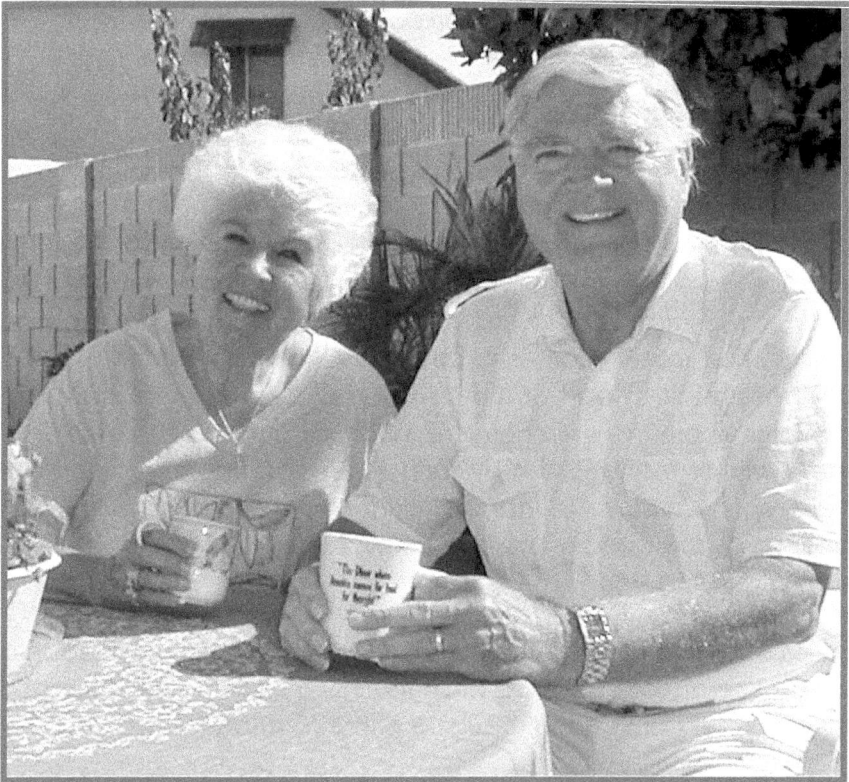

When I was growing up, legalism was prevalent. You were considered a Christian if you did or didn't do certain things, and that was "Bible thumped" into us. Before I was married, I wasn't allowed to wear makeup. In fact, the day I got married I didn't have any makeup on. So you can figure out how long ago that was. Understanding grace comes back to having wisdom. When I prayed for wisdom during the day, I expected God to show me what to do, not what others thought was right, but God himself.

I realize that we were legalistic on certain issues in that we didn't allow our kids to do this and that when we were raising them. They give me a hard time about it now and I look at them and say, "Well, you didn't turn out so bad!" There are certain areas that I gave them more leniency because they could handle it, but all in all, I stood firm out of love and the urgency to do God's will. I desired that they didn't have any wasted years. My goal was to keep them on the straight and narrow. I didn't want them to deviate and do things that they would regret in years to come. It was very challenging to trust them to the Lord to do His will.

Our kids could take advantage of Doc and me in some of our rules. But there were some laws that were the "Laws of the Medes and the Persians." My curfew was one of them. I never went to bed at night until my kids were in and they were all asleep. They knew I would be sitting on that old gold couch waiting for them when they came in. And I was. Another one was church. They could never miss church. My kids still remember Kandi throwing up in the car on the way to church, and we didn't turn around. We kept going. I don't remember it that way, but they all swear it is true. I guess we were very legalistic on that one. We were training our kids to be responsible and serve others. Our church relied on them to make it work. After all, Kenette was a Sunday school teacher, Kenton led the worship, and Kandi was in charge of the babies (of course, not on the day she was throwing up, when she had to stay in the ladies bathroom and sleep on the couch). Giving our children our trust and leadership in our church was positive because they felt like it was their ministry and that we valued their input.

Life Principle: Apply Grace Instead of Legalism
to Instill Spiritual Growth

Another area where we need to apply grace is in our own lives. We are often very hard on ourselves. We stop our own spiritual growth by focusing on what we did wrong. Although God has forgiven us, we have a hard time letting it go. If we don't apply grace to our own lives, we'll stay stuck in our spiritual growth.

❖ What are the rules and regulations about your spiritual growth that you're not sure whether they are from you or from the Word? Spend some time finding out from the Word if they are in line with what God says.

❖ Sometimes we get stuck focusing on our past, which keeps us from growing spiritually. Are there areas where you are stuck in your past or where you have thoughts that won't go away? Are there hurts you seem to rehash or people you need to forgive?

❖ Are there areas in your life as a wife and/or mother/grandmother/great grandmother where you need to apply grace rather than legalism?

Forgetting what lies behind and reaching forward to what lies ahead, I press on toward the goal for the prize of the upward call of God in Christ Jesus. – Phil. 3:13-14

Gain Wisdom

My theme song is to be reverent in the way I live and to ask God for His wisdom. I've done it for almost eighty years. As I mentioned before, every day I pray for wisdom before my feet ever hit the floor. Then during the day in situations where someone will call me and ask for advice, I don't give advice any more, I give suggestions if the person wants to hear them. Before I give a suggestion, I whisper in my brain, *Lord, give me wisdom to say the right thing and to respond to whatever they say in the right way.* James 1:5 says, *"If any of you lacks wisdom, let him ask of God, who gives to all liberally and without reproach, and it will be given to him."* Wisdom is one of the few things you don't have to work for. All you have to do is ask for it. It's so simple that I don't understand why everybody isn't banging the doors of heaven 24/7 asking for wisdom. None of us have wisdom in our own selves, and we all need it from the Lord.

Many try to pass off their own wisdom as being wisdom from the Lord. That just doesn't work! God knows what's going on inside us. We can't fool God. 1 Corinthians 3:18-22 says:

> *Let no one deceive himself. If anyone among you seems to be wise in this age, let him become a fool that he may become wise. For the wisdom of this world is foolishness with God. For it is written, "He catches the wise in their own craftiness;" and again, "The LORD knows the thoughts of the wise, that they are futile." Therefore let no one boast in men.*

How else can we get wisdom? In addition to asking for wisdom, we can also find it through fearing the Lord. This means reverence for God, not being afraid of Him. Too many preachers used to teach us to be so afraid of God that we would become legalistic in what we could or couldn't do to please Him. Psalm 111:10 says: *"The fear of the LORD is the beginning of wisdom; a good understanding have all those who do His commandments. His praise endures forever."*

Life Principle: Trade Your Worldly Wisdom for
God's Wisdom to Avoid Stumbling

How many times do we base our actions on our own insights, only to fall flat? Afterwards we ask God for His wisdom in the situation. It would be much easier if we always asked God for His wisdom and guidance first. Sometimes it seems foolish and we're hesitant to obey His guidance. But in the end, He knows what's best for us. It is my prayer to do what God wants me to do. Is it hard to put aside my own desire to do things my way? Yes! But I've learned in no way can my wisdom compare to God's wisdom.

❖ What is an example of when you knew God was telling you to do one thing and you ended up doing your own thing instead? Did you have to fail at that before you eventually followed God's guidance?

❖ In what area(s) of your life do you need to trade in your worldly wisdom for God's wisdom? When will you do it?

❖ In what circumstances do you have the most difficult time exhibiting God's wisdom?

He stores up sound wisdom for the upright; He is a shield to those who walk uprightly. –Proverbs 2:7

Discern God's Will

How does a person know what God has called him or her to do? Many Christians never find the answer to these questions. But it's not that hard.

I have based my life on John 7:17: *"If anyone wills to do His will, he shall know concerning the doctrine, whether it is from God or whether I speak on My own authority."* I could not have served God the way I have during my life if I didn't believe that He would show me what it was He wanted me to do. On the basis of God's word, He has promised to do that. That means, "Okay, God, I'm willing to do Your will. Now, the balls are in Your court. You have to show me what it is. I'm willing to do it. I've got the racket. I'm willing to serve it. I'm willing to do whatever you want me to do, but You have to show me what it is." Many times it has been difficult to know exactly which way God would have me turn. But if we are living according to God's Word, honestly asking God for wisdom and not trying to do our own will but sincerely being willing to do whatever it is He places before us, then God will show us what His will is.

We cannot say, "I don't know what God wants me to do." God's Word says He will show you what He wants you to do and He promises to do that. Psalm 25:4-5 says, *"Show me Your ways, O LORD; Teach me Your paths. Lead me in Your truth and teach me, For You are the God of my salvation; On You I wait all the day."*

I have relied on that verse many times in my life when I was not sure which way to go. I would say to the Lord, "I'm going to start out. If this is not Your way, then You close the door or open another window or show me which way You want me to go. But I'm going on the basis of Your Word that You would show me." Finding God's will is more than saying, "God, show me what to do." We need to diligently seek and move towards that which we feel God would have us to do.

Life Principle: Ask God What His Will is for You, and He *Will* Tell You.

The title of this chapter is Pursue Daily Spiritual Growth. This can't be done if we don't know what God wants us to do every day. God has a "big" picture of your life, as well as "daily" things He wants you to do.

❖ Are you aware of God's "big" picture for your life? What do you understand is God's will or vision for your life? Are you pursuing it?

❖ What about the ins and outs of daily living? Do you discern His will in the little moments throughout your day? What areas do you need to ask Him to provide further discernment?

❖ What are some of the "one anothers" mentioned in the New Testament we are all supposed to be doing? Are you doing them?

Trust in the LORD with all your heart, and lean not on your own understanding; In all your ways acknowledge Him, and He shall direct your path.
– Proverbs 3:5-6

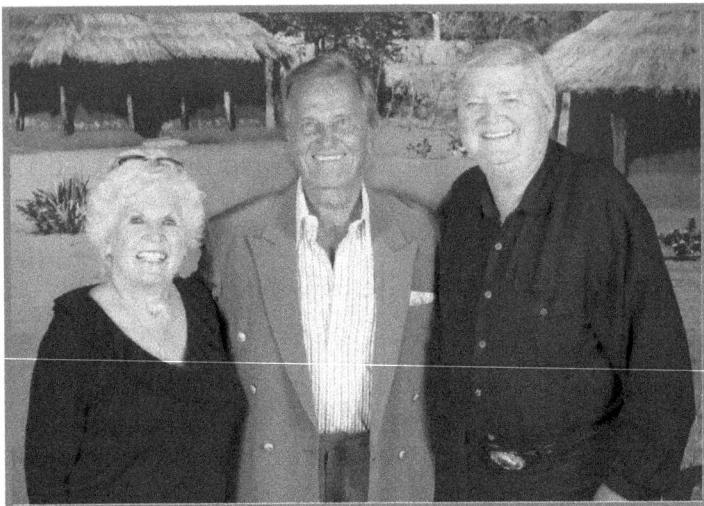
With Doc and entertainer Pat Boone

With Doc; "America's Rabbi" Shmuley Boteach;
author/commentator Dennis Prager; and Glen Megill

FOUR
4

Daily Living
for Christians

Living every day in the light of being a Christian requires focused attention. Since we live by a different standard than the world, our lives must reflect that. God calls us to be light in the darkness. How do we do that? Here are some of my suggestions.

Make Every Day Count

One of my children, Kenton, described me as having "biblical unquenchable optimism." I've always been a positive person, maybe because I woke up before my children and read the Word every morning. I always tried to be positive. Each day I went into their rooms and said, "This is the day the Lord has made, rejoice and be glad in it!" Many times I had pillows thrown at me because they did not like that I was singing and so cheerful. They would ask, "Do you have to sing in the morning?" But I was always optimistic in the mornings because I felt truly that the Lord had made the day. Happiness is a choice, and I chose (and still choose) to be happy.

Now at my age I realize how important this has been throughout my whole life. Especially now that I'm older, I recognize that I don't know how many days the Lord has left for me on this earth. I want each day to be as full as it can be in serving the Lord. I want to stay optimistic about what He is going to do in my life and about how I can be a blessing to those with whom I come into contact. Again happiness is a choice.

I'll talk more about being optimistic in the next chapter. But in order to make every day count, I have to choose the right attitude before I even get out of bed. Obviously the Lord has worked greatly in my life to draw me to Him as early as He did when I was a young child. However, even though He continues to draw me close to Him, it's my choice to respond. It's my choice to put on that positive attitude each morning. I've learned throughout my life that being positive is the best attitude to have and it gets good results. To live each day to its fullest, I can't walk around being gloomy all day, having "grumpy in my heart." I'm grateful that when I choose to be positive, God rewards me for it. After all, God is the most positive Person around!

Also it is very important to pick positive friends. How many times have you been around someone that brings you down? When you leave, you feel so oppressed. Maybe they have been gossiping or maybe they have been down on their husband or children or their life. Those people keep you looking down and focusing on the negative. They can't help you be an eagle that is soaring above the problems in life. God calls us to soar, and it is a choice. Who are you going to choose to be your friend? Someone focused on the world and all of the worldly problems or someone who helps you focus on the Lord and brings you up? Choose your friends wisely.

How does God reward me? He gives me joy and peace as I walk in His love and listen to the Holy Spirit guiding me. But it's so easy to get away walking in the Spirit. We should be careful not to say *yes* to too many things. When we do, we end up getting too frazzled and we can't be the right person that we should be. Even if you are even-tempered, getting involved in too many things can make you stressed.

We need to recognize what we can and cannot do and not try to do what someone else is doing. Because I have a lot of energy, even at my age, I can do certain things that maybe other people who are 87 are unable to do because they're not well enough. That doesn't mean I'm doing better than they are. It is just that I have the high energy level that allows me to work and be productive. So use the energy level that you have to accomplish the things He want on the day. God will give you strength. Don't push yourself beyond the limits of your energy or beyond your physical strength. Each person has different physical abilities that God has given.

To help me live every day to its fullest, every morning I would ask God what He wanted me to do that day. Then in the evening I would ask God if there was something that I missed during the day that He was trying to guide me to do. I always want to do what He wants me to do. But I won't know what that is if I don't ask Him every single day.

Life Principle: Make Every Day Count
If You Want to Live a Fulfilled Life

I hope by now you're picking up on the fact that I had to intentionally commit my time and actions to listen to God, to obey Him, and then to reap His blessings. You can have the same blessings in your life.

❖ Are you frazzled from doing too much every day? If so, what can you cut back on or delete from your schedule?

❖ Are you hearing from God every morning about what He wants you to do that day?

❖ Are you being you or are you trying to be like somebody else? God created you as a unique person. He knows your abilities as well as any lack. Ask Him to show you how to be the best person He wants you to be.

❖ Pick your friends wisely. Do you have negative friends? Don't waste your time with them. Choose people who help you focus on the Lord. Friends who help you soar!

My son (daughter), give attention to my words; Incline your ear to my sayings. Do not let them depart from your eyes; Keep them in the midst of your heart; For they are life to those who find them, And health to all their flesh. Keep your heart with all diligence, For out of it spring the issues of life. – Proverbs 4:20-23

Don't Live In The Past

God has been good to Doc and me in giving us good health, even though Doc has 22 stints. We have been very fortunate in being healthy most of our lives. Even today we are serving the Lord daily. Doc goes to work every day Monday through Thursday. On Fridays we bowl with our grandkids. Sundays he teaches the Bible class at church.

I mentor and I teach when I'm asked, and I count it a privilege. I don't ever want to say that whatever I did in the past is that important today. I want to find out what God wants me to do today, not stuck in the past.

I want to focus on today. I don't want to be stuck with guilt or blame or shame from yesterday's mistakes. So I CHOOSE to focus on today. I think it is important for us to live in forgiveness and move forward. Satan wants us to stay mired in yesterday's mistakes, but we have a forgiving God who doesn't remember what we did even yesterday when we have asked Him for forgiveness.

There are times I've noticed in some of my friends who are my age saying, "Remember when we did this, or remember when we did that?" Those are fine memories and they are good things to recall. However, they need to take the rear view mirror off of their lives and stop looking back. God calls us to ask ourselves, "What are we doing for God today?" This is the day the Lord has made we should rejoice and be glad in it. We should find out what God wants us to do **today**.

One of my New Year's resolutions last year was that every day I want to do something for someone else, whether it be a phone call or writing a little note or a word of encouragement to someone who I feel needs it. Taking the focus off ourselves changes our hearts and gets us out of a selfish focus.

My mother used to say, "A person wrapped up in their own self makes a mighty small package." If we are only thinking of me, myself, and I, and "What can I do for me," it isn't the best way to live. Some of the best days that we have ever enjoyed (and I'm sure the same is true with you) are when I've done things for other people or been a blessing to others. I know that God has led me in doing that. That's why I want to look forward to what God has for me today, tomorrow, and for as long as He allows me to be here.

Life Principle: To Fully Live Today, You Must Let Go of Your Past

---

When we let go of our past, this also includes the good things. If we're dwelling upon how good things used to be, we are not living fully in the present.

❖ Are there things in your past—both good and bad—that keep you from fully living today? What are they?

❖ In order to change your thinking from the past, you must

have a future to look forward to. What is God asking you to do today? What is His big picture for your life?

❖ What can you do to reach out in love and service of others every day?

Not that I have already attained, or am already perfected; but I press on, that I may lay hold of that for which Christ Jesus has also laid hold of me. Brethren, I do not count myself to have apprehended; but one thing I do, forgetting those things which are behind and reaching forward to those things which are ahead, I press toward the goal for the prize of the upward call of God in Christ Jesus. –Philippians 3:12-14

Leave a Legacy One Day at a Time

Leaving a legacy to the next generation is a tough issue these days. Many grandparents feel there is not much they can do to influence their grandchildren. I'd like to encourage you grandparents and great-grandparents that you can impact the lives of the young ones in your lives and leave your legacy for future generations.

My grandchildren and great-grandchildren would speak well of this heritage because I am leaving a legacy with them. Even today I put their schedules ahead of mine. When my great-grandchildren are having any sporting event or another activity, I love showing up for them! By letting them know they come before anything else, other than God and my husband, I let them know that what they are doing is very important to me. I want to support them and be their best cheerleader. I think that grandparents miss a lot by not being there for their grandkids.

Some people feel they have paid their dues by raising their children, and that now that they are grandparents, it is their time in life to focus on themselves. They think they'll be more satisfied by taking vacations rather than investing themselves in the lives of their grandchildren. I don't agree. I love to travel with my husband, and

42

there is plenty of time for that, but I love to be there for my grandkids and great-grandchildren.

I personally don't ever feel I've paid my dues. I don't feel that my dues will be paid until I go out feet first on my death bed. And that's when your dues are paid, when you're with the Lord. To me I enjoy being with my family and my family has always been top priority to me. That's because I enjoy being with them and seeing what they're doing and seeing how God is answering my prayers through them.

I know a lot of people don't feel that way. They feel that they've paid their dues and that they should be able to live for themselves. I'm not saying they're wrong, but that's not where I find my joy. Throughout the Word, God tells us to pass along to the next generation God's truths so that they will know how to live godly lives. Psalm 78:4 speaks about this:

> We will not hide them from their children, telling to the generation to come the praises of the LORD, and His strength and His wonderful works that He has done.

What better way to pass along God's truths than by being a living example to our grandchildren and great-grandchildren? When we put aside our own agenda and reach out to loved ones, God blesses us beyond what we could ever expect.

Life Principle: Lay Aside Your Desires and Leave a Legacy by Loving Others and God

---

❖ How are you putting the lives of others above your own desires?

❖ What can you change in your life to have more impact in the lives of those you love?

❖ Are your life and your words demonstrating God's love toward others?

And remember the words of the Lord Jesus, that He said, "It is more blessed to give than to receive." –Acts 20:3 5

Maintain Balance in Your Life

Without having balance in disciplining the kids, putting your husband first, and being a servant working in the church, you can end up without having any energy left. Our responsibility is first to God, second to our husbands, and third to our families. Then we can branch out into other activities like teaching Sunday school, working in the church, and using the talents God has given us in the church. But I think a VERY IMPORTANT obligation we have is to train our own children.

Once Doc was away at a prophecy conference, and I had been staying up until three o'clock in the morning trying to paint and redecorate his office to surprise him. With the kids, I couldn't get much done during the day. Because I had been up most nights with my project, I evidently looked like death warmed over when I met him at the airport. He said, "Had a rough time, of it, huh?" I said, "Yes." And he said, "Lolo, I so appreciate you! Did you ever think that if every mother led their children to the Lord like you did, if every mother was faithful in rearing their kids, my job would be so much easier?" He thanked me for how hard I was working with our children (and that was before he saw the office I had redecorated).

Doc was right. Can you imagine how much better our world would be if moms were careful and took time to train their children in the ways of the LORD?

His thank you and his words of affirmation made me feel like a million bucks. I had spent the whole week with the kids. They had been sick, and I had been working hard to deal with them all being sick at the same time. When Doc called on the telephone, he asked, "How are things going?" I said, "The kids are a little sick, but they are all right and we are praying for you." I tried not to complain so he would not feel guilty for being away. He was grateful because he could concentrate on the conference and not feel badly. That is one example that I remember of how I tried to show my husband that he was first and how I strived daily to put my husband before our kids.

To keep balance in our own lives, it's important that we exercise too. I love tennis. I enjoyed playing tennis up until just a few years ago, but I didn't let it stand in the way of me taking care of my kids when they were younger. I didn't let it stop me from doing what I felt I should do for God. I used to call it my tennis evangelism. I was able to lead a couple of ladies to the Lord and always invited them to church through that. I enjoyed it myself. I miss it, but when I blew out a knee and a shoulder because of the game, my kids made me hang up my racquet!

If you have young kids and your day has been very stressful taking care of them, you need to realize that you may not have the time or energy to make yourself look like Wonder Woman when your husband comes home from work.

I think it's important that we look attractive for our husbands. I have a friend who will only wear sweat suits, and when her husband comes home, she hasn't even combed her hair. I have talked to her. She always uses the excuse that she is overweight, and she is not going to invest in clothes until she loses weight. This has been going on for close to 47 years! Make your husband feel special and that he is important to you. I used to try to have the kids cleaned up when Doc came home, and I tried to have dinner on the table. I was lucky I didn't have to work when my children were young, only later in their lives. I don't know how the women do it today, with babies and work and juggling day care. It sounds exhausting! I pray for my girls I mentor that when they are going through tough times, God will give them strength.

I know that many of the moms these days have image issues, feeling the pressure from either their peers or their spouses to look good, and they have a hard time making that part of their day. I suggest they talk to their husbands and find out what is really important. Then try to make that a priority.

There's a great emphasis on weight today. Women want to be skinny and get stressed out when they don't have the time to do whatever is necessary to achieve that "perfect image." Again, we have to look at our lives and bring balance to them.

An exercise plan should be a priority. As I've said, I walk and pray in the mornings. Do I always feel like doing it? No! I used to quote that verse to myself, *"To him who knows to do good and does not do it, to him it is sin"* (James 4:17). I would tell myself, "Get your tush out of bed and go walk and exercise!" Once I did it, I felt better. It is important that we exercise for our health so that we are well rounded (or so that we don't get too well rounded)!

Life Principle: Live a Balanced Life
So God Can Bless Others through You

❖ Looking at the key areas of your life—physical, mental, social, and spiritual—are you out of balance? Describe it and list how you can bring your life back into balance.

❖ Who do you look up to as a model of the Christian life? Can you identify how he or she is able to maintain balance in their life?

❖ Are you overly concerned about your weight and

appearance? Have you discussed with your spouse what he expects from you? Many times we think our husbands thinks one way, but when we ask, we learn he thinks differently.

Live in Peace and Joy

"Let the peace of God rule in your heart" (Colossians 3:15). You have a choice of whether you have peace in your soul or not. *"Faith comes by hearing and hearing by the word of God"* (Romans 10:17). We get faith through the Word of God. We get peace as we give ourselves to the Lord. When we do the right things, peace floods our soul. I have real peace in my heart. I can work on maintaining peace and joy by thinking on "whatever is good and right" and by trying to act accordingly. I still choose to be happy even though it is not easy now that my body is not what it once was and my eyes are going. I stay grateful for all of the good years I have had with my eyes and my body.

Peace, to me, is being satisfied with the way things are and not trying to change them. It also includes contentment and godliness. Many women don't understand what peace means. They say, "I had a peace in my heart about this or about that," then they make decisions based on what they want.

Colossians 3: 15 says: *"Let the peace of God rule in your hearts."* He's like an umpire in a game when he says "safe." When you make a decision where you sought God's will, then you can have that satisfaction that you made the right decision. If you don't have that satisfaction or you don't have the confirmation of peace in your heart, then re-examine your actions.

Joy is also a choice. Surround yourself with people who have peace and joy. Stay away from negative people so you don't become negative. I used to tell the kids that people think of you by the company you keep, and it is important to have friends that also have the same values that you have in life as well as the same joys in life that you have.

I have a friend that I love to talk to because she's always up and happy. I have another friend that I love dearly, but she complains all the time. She doesn't have that much to complain about, but she has developed the habit of complaining. She's a lovely person, and I love her, but she complains. With another friend, we both feel better when we get off the phone after talking. I'm sure it's because we have a positive attitude towards our children, our husbands, and our grandchildren.

How do we develop peace and joy? We can't be at peace if we're anxious or fearful. We have to learn to turn our worries over to the Lord. *"Be anxious for nothing, but in everything by prayer and supplication, with thanksgiving, let your requests be made known to God; and the peace of God, which surpasses all understanding, will guard your hearts and minds through Christ Jesus"* (Philippians 4:6-7). Sometimes if the Lord doesn't work in a situation as quickly as we want Him to, we end up taking back that anxiety and stress and trying to work things out in our own wisdom. I have often tried to help God, and I realize He does not need my help.

Life Principle: Turn Your Cares Over to the Lord to Receive Peace and Joy

❖ What counterfeit peace have you been looking to? For example, have you looked for peace through people, circumstances, possessions, pleasure, or escape?

❖ What anxieties and/or fears can you bring to the Lord and allow Him to handle?

❖ With the Holy Spirit inside you, you already have joy. Will you choose to display that joy today? What actions demonstrate you are joyful?

Peace I leave with you, My peace I give to you; not as the world gives do I give to you. Let not your heart be troubled, neither let it be afraid. –John 14:27

FIVE

Create Life-Impacting
Relationships

Relationships can be boring or exciting. It all depends upon what *you* put into them. All of the principles presented in these chapters affect the quality of your relationships. Here are some guidelines I try to live by that improve any relationship I'm in.

Choose Your Attitudes

Our attitudes make or break relationships. It's important to be a positive person and to find the best in those with whom you live and those that you meet along the way. People are very grateful when we compliment them, and it brings out the best in them.

My attitude is that of expecting great things and expecting my kids to turn out great. I never thought they wouldn't. I always expected the best of them, and I always tried to bring out the best in them. In addition to the affirmations I mentioned before, I always told them they could never do anything that would cause them not to be welcome at home. I might not always agree with them, but I want them to know they are always welcome at home. I told them many times, "I know God has a great plan for your life, and all you have to do is follow it and ask for wisdom."

Trusting God has eliminated much worry in my life. You can either worry about a situation or trust God with it. This positive attitude of trusting God helps us, and it also impacts everyone involved. Like negative attitudes can influence us and others, our positive attitude of trusting God can influence others.

My attitude of trusting God came from seeing Him work over and over in my life and in the lives of my husband and children. It also came from spending so much time reading the Word and praying to God.

When I find myself in a situation that is negative or where I have an opportunity to be negative and complain, I remember I have a choice. I can think only about "me" and how good it would feel to complain, or I can think about how having a positive attitude will help those around me. Then I ask the Lord to help me do what He wants me to do.

Life Principle: The Attitude You Choose
Impacts Everything You Do

❖ What bad attitude do you need to get rid of? How can you replace it with a positive one that pleases God?

❖ If you're a complainer, take a pen and paper and write some positive statements you can say the next time you feel like complaining. By having this list ahead of time, you can be aware of the option to speak positively instead of negatively.

❖ Want a real eye opener? Take a 30-day fast from complaining and being negative. The goal is to go 30 straight days without verbally complaining. If you blow it on day six, start all over again. Pretty soon you'll notice the negative self-talk also begins to go away.

Finally, brethren, whatever is true, whatever is honorable, whatever is right, whatever is pure, whatever is lovely, whatever is of good repute, if there is any excellence and if anything worthy of praise, dwell on these things. –Philippians 4:8

Stop Listening To Gossip

Today many women complain about their husbands or about their friends or their circumstances. I don't listen to gossip because it is bound to affect how I think about that person in the future. When you've heard something negative, it's bound to come into your mind again.

When I hear someone who's starting to say something unkind about a friend or about someone that I know, I try to remember the good things that that person said about them.

Or if someone starts to gossip, I say, "You know let's get together with her. We really need to talk about this, because I want everyone that's involved in it to discuss it. I don't want to listen to one side of the story. I wouldn't listen to her talking about you, and I don't want to hear you talking about her unless we all get together and can solve the problem." I also ask, "Am I part of the problem?" If I'm not part of the problem, or if I can't solve the problem, then I don't want to listen to it. I'm not unkind in how I say this. I found that it's not good to listen to gossip, and God is not pleased with it.

When you listen to something negative that affects you, it's bound to affect your feelings toward that person and how you act with that person. Also you've given the person permission to complain. It's never helpful to be a complainer or to allow another person to complain.

I know it's not easy to jump in and stop someone from gossiping, but someone's got to do it! Ladies are so concerned about what others think about them that they don't do what God wants them to do. God wants us to speak up and assert ourselves by stopping ungodly behavior. My goal is to please God, not the person I'm talking to.

Gossiping happens all around us. We watch it all the time. On TV shows, the news, and when we're in a crowd, we hear others gossiping. Can we completely escape it? No, but we can limit it by not taking part and by intervening in areas that are under our control.

Life Principle: Stop Gossiping and Stop the Strife

❖ If you have been guilty of gossiping about others, ask God to forgive you. Also ask Him to help you change starting right now.

❖ Is there someone in your life who is always gossiping around you? Determine ahead of time how you will handle that situation the next time it comes up. Will you ask her to not talk about the person without that person present so that the two of you can help that person instead of adding to the problem?

❖ Who can you ask to hold you accountable to stop your own gossiping? Tell that person of your desire and give her/him permission to confront you when you start to gossip. When you are confronted, respond by simply saying, "Thank you" and change the topic.

Fire goes out without wood, and quarrels disappear when gossip stops. – Proverbs 26:20

Love Your Neighbors

One way we can love our neighbors it to literally be kind to the people who live near us. It's important to smile and be a good neighbor. I'm always careful that I don't make noise after a certain hour. Even when the kids were younger and they were throwing parties, I would go next door and say, "The kids are going to be having a party, and we might be a little noisy but we will be quiet by this time," and ask if that would be okay. I tried to cover the bases beforehand so that I wasn't offensive to my neighbors. Now I have a dog that barks, and I tell my neighbor, "I'm doing the best I can with that dog," and I bring the dog indoors. Recently, I had the opportunity to reach out to new neighbors, bringing them banana bread and our church bulletin. It gave me a chance to ask if they attended service anywhere. So I try to be a good neighbor even in the smaller things. When our neighbors see we are different from others, we can influence those around us and give glory to God for showing us how to live.

Life Principle: Love Your Neighbor and
You Are Loving God

❖ Do you even know who your neighbor is? You can meet them by taking something to them, perhaps something you baked or a copy of your church bulletin, and you can invite them to your church next Sunday.

❖ While you're meeting your neighbors, ask them if there is anything you can pray about for them. Also give them your phone number, and ask them to call you if there is anything you can help them with.

Jesus said to him, "'You shall love the LORD your God with all your heart, with all your soul, and with all your mind.' This is the first and great commandment. And the second is like it: 'You shall love your neighbor as yourself.' On these two commandments hang all the Law and the Prophets." – Matthew 22:37-40

Get Rid of Bitterness

Bitterness keeps people away from you. It puts a negative taint on your life. It grows and at first we don't recognize what's happening. Some people are just bitter people because they've let it take over their lives. When we do this, we're only hurting ourselves. When we're bitter toward someone else, we're not hurting them. They're probably not even cognizant of the fact that we're bitter towards them.

Bitterness destroys a person. Have you ever noticed that women my age or older either look bitter or they have the light of the Lord in their face? They have a glow about them and have peace. I'm grateful that God gives us contentment when we walk in His way.

How do you get rid of bitterness if you think you've got it? Bitterness develops when you fail to forgive someone who hurt you. Your heart becomes hardened toward that person and also toward similar situations with others in your life. Only through forgiving that person will you begin to soften your heart and allow the bitterness to disappear. Forgiving someone doesn't mean they get away with what happened; the Lord will deal with that. Forgiveness is for my benefit. And once I've forgiven a person, I also need to quit remembering and talking about any hurt from that situation. I've got to move on with my life.

Life Principle: Forgive Others and Bitterness
No Longer Holds You in Bondage to Sin

❖ Do you know if you are bitter? Ask those closest to you if they see you as being bitter (and be prepared for the answer). How does that show up in your words and actions?

- ❖ If you are bitter, what incident from your past keeps popping up in your mind and gets you upset, or what do you constantly talk about?

- ❖ Now, forgive that person right now. You can't wait until your emotions tell you it's time to forgive them because that time never comes.

- ❖ Part of forgiveness is to never bring up that incident again (and this includes in your thoughts). Instead, every time this incident comes up, pray that God will bless that person today. Then move on in your life.

And do not grieve the Holy Spirit of God, by whom you were sealed for the day of redemption. Let all bitterness, wrath, anger, clamor, and evil speaking be put away from you, with all malice. And be kind to one another, tenderhearted, forgiving one another, even as God in Christ forgave you. – Ephesians 4:30-32

Set Boundaries

How do you choose the right friends and distance yourself from those you feel are a negative influence? What if you have a family member who is negative or likes to gossip and you feel like you're stuck with them?

If I had negative friends, I would not be around them continuously. If I can't help them or if I'm not doing anything good for them, I would limit my time with them because I don't want that to bring myself down. I have to protect myself from allowing negativity into my life.

But with a family member that you're stuck with, it is difficult. You can mention to them that you wish they wouldn't complain or talk to them about it and try to make it better.

You need to set boundaries. I have not been the best at this. One of the things I'm still learning today is to set certain boundaries. In the ministry, we always accepted any invitation that was given to us, because as a minister we would be expected to do that. We don't do that anymore. We have set boundaries and we only spend social time with those we choose to. There was a couple that we knew and they were continually fighting with each other. We just chose not to be around them anymore.

To have good, positive relationships in your life, you have to be intentional about whom you spend time with as well as limiting negative input into your life. This is why we set boundaries.

Did Jesus set boundaries? Yes! Several times when He was about to perform a miracle, He put out of the house all those who did not believe so He could heal a person or raise that person from the dead. He kept the disciples who did believe close so that He could perform the acts He said He was going to do.

Sometimes parents need to set boundaries for our children when they're too young to know how to set their own boundaries about the friends they choose. It's important that parents take an active role in helping their children choose the right friends. I'll go into this more in the chapter on being a mother.

Another influence on the choices our children make will be the movies and TV shows they watch and what they can access on the Internet. Being a parent today is much tougher than it was when I was younger. The movies have gotten more violent and sexually explicit, which dramatically impacts how children interact with others.

The violent themes of movies, as well as the negative words in the music children hear, leads them to seek out friends who focus on the dark side of life. Parents today must take a very active role in screening what goes into their children's lives and minds. If all the children receive is darkness, how dark it is! But when we shed God's light into their lives, it overcomes the darkness.

Remember, we are in a spiritual battle, especially when it comes to raising godly children. Even though they grumbled at times when I woke my children with my cheerful phrase, I shed God's light on them before their feet ever touched the ground. I couldn't wait until evening time to influence them.

Setting boundaries is not only to keep out the negative influence; it is also to let the good influences into our lives.

Life Principle: Setting Boundaries
Keeps Satan's Influence Out

❖ To know where to set boundaries, you have to know what bad influences you want to keep out of your life as well as the positive ones you want to develop in your family. Write a list of what you know is currently in your life that is harmful and what you need to get out of your life.

❖ Now write a list of the good influences you want in your life and your family.

❖ How can you begin to implement items on each list? Which ones will you work on first? If you're married, have a family meeting and get everyone involved. Paint a picture for them of how much better the family life will be when these items are either removed or brought into their lives.

Keep your heart with all diligence, For out of it spring the issues of life. – Proverbs 4:23

With Doc and Tom and Vickie Sanders

In the studio during a radio broadcast

SIX

Making a Marriage Last

D oc and I have been married for 65 years. Why do some marriages last so long? In addition to what has been discussed so far in this book, God has certain principles for marriage that play out differently. It requires commitment and lots of give-and-take.

Attitudes in Marriage

Our attitudes make or break our marriages. Many people feel entitled to complain. While there are always things to complain about, there are always ways to be positive. Again, attitude is a choice. In fact, it's a command from the Lord to focus upon the positive in life, even if our spouse is negative at the moment.

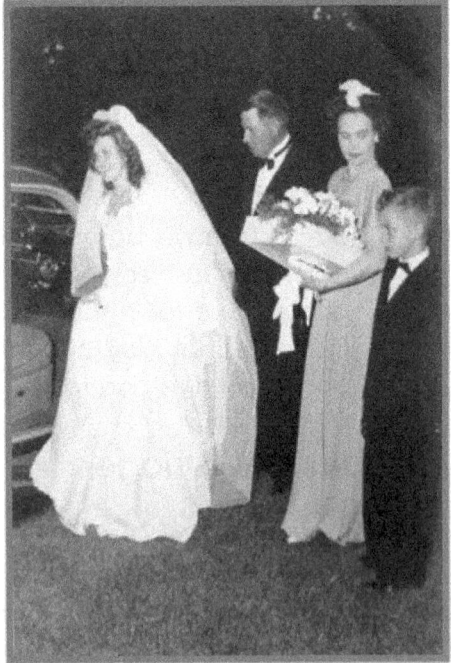

I always believed that my husband could do almost anything, and I tried to make him feel that way. I've mentioned how I encouraged him in his preaching, but if I had a suggestion for the sermon, I would wait to express it until later during the week. I would say something like, "I was just thinking about your sermon last week and I was wondering what you thought about 'this'"? I tried to be helpful, not critical.

To ensure my husband's success, I stayed positive in my encouragement. I have also always been there for him. When I'm asked to do something, I do it to the best of my ability without complaining.

We never allowed pouting or complaining in our home. We wanted to be a home where each person could be positive. Even when the kids were dealing with each other, I would talk to them and say, "Don't complain, but enjoy it." As I am a naturally fun person, I always tried to be a fun person with Doc. When we didn't have enough money to go on a date night alone every week, we took the kids with us. That didn't put a damper on our date, and we always had fun.

Sometimes husbands do things that we don't like. How do we handle that? You have to think the best about him. Don't concentrate on his negative attributes, but concentrate on the positive ones. Focus on the reasons why you married him in the first place and express appreciation for the reasons why he is a good husband or a good father. Stress those characteristics in your mind.

The Bible says, "*Whatever things are true, whatever things are noble, whatever things are just, whatever things are pure, whatever things are lovely, whatever things are of good report, if there is any virtue and if there is anything praiseworthy—meditate on these things*" (Philippians 4:8). It's important to think on the right things. If we let our minds go the wrong way and concentrate on what is not good, that affects our life negatively and we will say things that we shouldn't say.

It is a self-control issue. The more you control your thoughts, the easier it becomes. *"For as he thinks in his heart, so is he"* (Proverbs 23:7). Whatever you dwell on in your mind impacts how you feel in your relationship. You probably have noticed that when you think godly thoughts, it affects your actions in a positive way. I often quote Scripture to myself to control my thoughts.

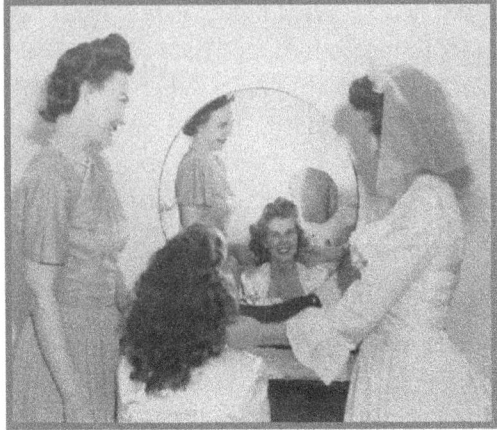

When I went in for an operation recently, I quoted the verse, *"Fear not, for I am with you; be not dismayed for I am your God. I will strengthen you, yes, I will help you, I will uphold you with My righteous right hand"* (Isaiah 41:10). What more can I ask? I quoted it over and over again. I quoted other Scriptures too, *"Be steadfast, immovable, always abounding in the work of the Lord"* (1 Corinthians 15:58). It doesn't say "sometimes you abound in it" or "if you feel like it, you abound in it," but it says to always abound in it. Does that mean you always feel great? No. But when you don't, quoting Scripture will help your attitude change.

Sometimes I start to sing hymns and praises. As I think about that, I remember how I used to sing solos when we were first married. But now, I sing to keep my positive focus which shapes our lives, the life of my husband, and the lives of our children, and the lives of the people we have contact with.

Life Principle: The Attitude You Choose
Sets the Tone of Your Marriage

❖ Look at the last two weeks in your marriage. What has been your attitude?

- ❖ When tough times come, what can you think, do or say to keep yourself in a positive frame of mind?

- ❖ You must be proactive in your relationship with your husband, not merely reactive. What words or actions can you take to be proactive?

- ❖ Do you have the three attitudes that hurt any marriage: being unforgiving, being selfish, and being un-teachable?

- ❖ Do you have the three attitudes necessary for a great marriage: trust, appreciation, and acceptance?

  An excellent wife is the crown of her husband.
  – Proverbs 12:4

Submissiveness

I do think that I am a submissive wife; however, I do know when to talk and when not to talk. I think that saves me a lot of trouble. I also know that sometimes you need to "save it for the big ones."

The word submissive has been misused. It doesn't mean being walked on or being trampled on or not having an opinion. I have strong opinions in certain areas, and I express them. I work with Doc, and we broadcast every week together through the World Bible Society, even at our age. When I walk into that office, I ask him if he wants my suggestions. If he wants them, I give them to him; if he doesn't, I don't. At home, I would generally not ask, but make the suggestion. I try not to be a person who is overbearing in making my opinion the only one that matters. I'm always willing to listen.

Today, when you mention the word submission, most of the generation bristles and thinks, "I'm not going to be submissive!" But the comparison can be made to a company with a CEO, the person in charge. Submission is getting the proper perspective of your family. Being submissive is not being less than or inferior to, but it's realizing our place.

A family needs a CEO and if you think in those terms, the husband is the CEO. However, we have our responsibilities too, whether it is the chief financial officer, or another position. None of these roles is less than. Many people think submission means being less than, but I don't feel less than my husband because I'm submissive. Rather I am enhancing our family. I'm also bringing out the best in him as a person and supporting his position.

I've heard that many of today's young women have a hard time submitting to their husbands if they feel like their husbands are asking them to do something that they don't agree with. How should they respond to this?

My daughter Kenette, who is a psychologist, said, "Mom, we're always entitled to our feelings." If I feel that something is unfair or I don't feel that it is the thing that I should do right now, we need to speak up in the right way with the right attitude and in the right tone of voice and say "No, I'm not going to do that."

You can get what you want without being difficult to get along with. It means to learn to live as a family in the way that God ordained it. God did ordain our husbands to be the head of the family. That's timeless and how God ordered it, and I want to fit into God's plan.

The outcome of being submissive is a good family. I practice what the Bible tells us to do, and that is by daily doing what God would have me do. There's no particular formula for attaining it. It's doing it every day. Just do it.

Life Principle: Submission to Our Husbands Pleases God and Brings Order to Our Marriages

---

❖ Are there areas in your life where you feel you need to be submitting to your husband, but you're not? If so, what are the reasons for not submitting?

- ❖ Do you and your husband have the correct perspective on what biblical submission is? If not, can you meet with your pastor to gain further insight?

- ❖ Is there an older couple who you admire who is living a godly marriage? Can you establish a friendship with the lady for the purpose of gaining wisdom from her on how to handle situations as they arise in a marriage?

Wives, submit to your own husbands, as to the Lord.
– Ephesians 5:22

Loving Your Husband

Love is shown through our actions as well as the words we speak. We need to show our love for our husbands. We also need to tell our husbands that we love them. Many times it's like in *Fiddler On The Roof:* I wash his clothes, I clean the house, I take care of his kids. Of course, he knows that I love him. No, he doesn't! He needs to be told so.

This is the reason why husbands go elsewhere for attention, because they're not getting proper attention at home. We should tell them we love them. We should show it in our actions when we're with them. I always take my husband's hand and hold it. I have a friend who is a minister's wife, and she says, "How come you take your husband's hand? He should take your hand. I won't take my husband's hand." Well, they never hold hands! Even today sometimes Doc will do it, but I often take his hand first. I'll put my hand on his knee while he is driving. I think showing affection lets him know I love him. We need to express our love in action as well as with our words.

This also carries over into what happens at night. The Song of Solomon has much to say about that. We make sure that we are partners with our husbands in that we enjoy what God has ordained for us. We should enjoy sex with our husbands, and be the sex partner to him that God intended us to be.

❖ Do you have special ways of showing your husband that you love him?

❖ How often do you purposely do something specific to show your husband you love him?

❖ If you need ideas on how to show your husband that you love him, ask him!

❖ Sometimes words or actions that you think express your love are different from the way he would like to be shown love. A good book to help you understand your differences in how you enjoy receiving and expressing love is *The Five Love Languages: How to Express Heartfelt Commitment To Your Mate* by Gary Chapman.

My little children, let us not love in word or in tongue, but in deed and in truth. –1 John 3:18

Following God's Direction in Your Marriage

Part of being submissive carries over to denying our own interests and following our husband's into ministry or on the path he chooses in life rather than our husbands following us and what we're doing.

When we were living in Minneapolis, Ken wanted to study with Dr. Cooper. My folks felt that going to California was like going to hell. His folks felt the same way. Even our friends agreed. But he felt he could never be the minister he wanted to be if he did not study under Dr. Cooper. Against all odds, friends, and family, we came to California so that he could study with Dr. Cooper.

Ken left every Monday morning at five o'clock and did not come back until late Tuesday night. He studied all day Monday and all day Tuesday with Dr. Cooper for eight years to gain insights from him. Because that was important to him, I agreed and supported him. I didn't have the same desire to study with Dr. Cooper that he did. I also didn't feel that Dr. Cooper was as brilliant as Ken felt he was. But I agreed to go because that's what I felt God wanted me to do.

What if my husband asked me to follow him even if I felt it was not a biblical path, but he was interpreting it that way? This presents a difficulty because it's either biblical or not; either its right or it's not. If it's not right, I wouldn't choose that course. To me, that would be going against what God wants me to do.

Life Principle: Trusting God's Guidance
for Your Marriage Brings Contentment

❖ Are you fighting God's direction in your marriage? Have you submitted your concern to the Lord?

❖ If you feel that your husband wants to go in an ungodly direction in his life and wants you to support him and follow him, can the two of you speak to your pastor about this situation?

As for God, His way is perfect; The word of the LORD is proven; He is a shield to all who trust in Him. – II Samuel 22:3-1

SEVEN

Be a Godly Mother

Being a godly mother does not happen by accident. It takes being intentional and disciplined in choosing what is right in every situation.

Intentional Activities

Why is it important to have intentional activities? If you want a loving family with a strong foundation that provides structure which will not be easily torn apart, you must decide to create it.

Previously you read about how we created a home where our children's friends were always welcome and we wanted to get to know them so we could help them choose good influences. Another way to be involved in my children's lives was to know what their schedules were. My children were involved in athletics and other activities after school. In order to support them, I had to intentionally find out what activities were coming up, what time and at what location so I could plan out my weekly schedule. My children's activities were a high priority in my schedule.

As my children got into their teens, they didn't always want me to be at their activities, but I wanted to be there. When I cheered louder than any of the other parents there, it may have embarrassed my kids, but I didn't care. I wanted my kids to know that I loved them, that I believed in them, and that I was always there to cheer them on.

At one point, we had moved to a new community where we didn't know anyone. I saw how it was beginning to negatively affect my kids. There was this other family that I saw in church who Ken and I knew from our college days. They were a solid Christian family and I respected them. I went to them and developed a relationship with them, and after a couple of weeks, I said to them, "We have no family, will you be family for us?" And they said yes. They became an extended family for many years to come and their children were able to become great friends with our children. Doc writes more about this relationship in a later chapter.

With my mother

While choosing the activities I needed to be intentional on, I needed to recognize that I should not be overbearing and to remember what my children wanted to do with their lives, not what I wanted them to do. Their choice of careers had to be theirs, not mine. I helped them see the possible results of their upcoming choices and took everything to God in prayer.

As mentioned before, my prayer walk every morning was an intentional activity. Although what I prayed was behind the scenes, they knew I was praying for them. It had a significant impact on each of them. Almost every day I asked them how I could pray for them.

It was very important to me that my children understood the Bible and knew how to apply its principles. Doc will discuss our dinnertime devotions in chapter 9. To accomplish this, I had to be disciplined to make it a priority.

Life Principle: Building a Godly Family
Requires Goals with Intentional Activities

❖ What intentional activities are you currently doing with your family?

❖ What intentional activities do you want to add? Why? What is the underlying characteristic that it will develop in you and your family?

❖ Being intentional may require you to eliminate some of your current activities. If this is necessary, what are you going to give up? Starting when?

The wise woman builds her house. –Proverbs 14:1

Loving and Disciplining Your Children

We married young, and I wanted to have children. We still had two years to finish school so we couldn't have them right away. For the next three years, I put Doc through seminary. When Mark came into our life and God saw fit to take him home when he was six months old, it was a very difficult time. Our challenges caused us to grow. The doctor told us that often the death of a child drives couples apart because they blame each other when a child dies. Ken and I stayed together in this difficulty and as soon as the doctors said we could, we had another child.

Our children have always been a blessing to us, and we were so grateful to have them. They've been challenging at times, but they've always been a blessing. Even today I look forward to sitting in church with Kandi and Kenette as we listen to Kenton preach.

Because Kenette was the oldest, I was harder on her. I didn't want to make a mistake. As a first-time mother, I didn't know exactly how to raise my child. I always read, *"Train up a child in the way he should go and when he is old he will not depart from it"* (Proverbs 22:6). My goal was that my children would not depart from us during those years between their teenage years and their older years. I wanted to enjoy them every day of my life.

By being an intentional parent and living my life day-by-day as a consistent Christian, I told them what they could do and what they couldn't do. Looking at a part of the above Bible verse it says, *"train up the child in the way he should go. . . ."* it does not say "maybe train them" or "ask them what they want to do" or "let them do exactly what they want to do." Sometimes I see mothers in the store who allow their children to take the lead. But the verse says, *you* train them, to make the rules in the home and make sure they follow them.

I have always tried to disciple our children through being there for them and practicing the atttitudes and actions that I've discussed in this book. Helping our children understand God's love for them and our love for them adds balance to their lives. If we disciplined them without balancing it with love, they would be on the path toward rebellion.

You must also be self-disciplined in how you discipline. When you say you are going to discipline your child, you need to follow through and be consistent. You cannot tell the child she cannot do something for a week and then one day let her do it. If she is to be grounded for a certain amount of time, you need to stick to it. Decide what is fair discipline. Sometimes I asked my daughter, "What do you feel is right in this situation? Do you know that what you did was wrong? Should we take the car away? What do you feel is the right amount of time (to take the car way)?" Don't give in! Discipline has no affect if we do not stick to our word.

Life Principle: Raising Godly Children Requires A Balance of Love and Discipline

---

❖ Look at your recent attempts to discipline your child. Who was in control? If you were not in control, what can you do different next time so you are in control?

❖ Are you consistent in carrying through with implementing the rules in your house and the consequences for breaking those rules? Does your child know the rules?

❖ Do you have a balance of love and discipline in dealing with your children? If you're not sure, ask your children (if they're old enough).

Train up a child in the way he should go, And when he is old he will not depart from it. – Proverbs 22:6

Involvement in Children's Lives

As a mother I would do anything to ensure my children's success. As I've mentioned before, I would always attend my children's events whenever possible. I'm sure my kids thought I was crazy at times!

One time I was at my granddaughter, Holiday's, C.I.F. volleyball game. I was cheering so loudly that I began to choke. They had to stop the game and call the paramedics for me.

Another time, I was cheering Holiday on while she was running in a C.I.F. track meet. I got so excited that I actually ran out onto the track and ran the last 100 yards with her! I looked great in my satin hot pink, striped jumpsuit with hot pink boots! The judges had to escort me off the field. They did it with such grace because of my age. What they didn't know is that I could probably have beaten half of the runners on the track! Fortunately it didn't disqualify Holiday from the race.

My enthusiasm and zeal rubbed off on Holiday. We were both spectators at an event recently, and I saw how she was cheering for her kids as loudly as I used to cheer for her. It was such a blessing to see my granddaughter go all out to support her kids and do what I loved to do for her.

Kenette used to say "You are the best cheerleader we have!" My children, my ten grandchildren, and my great grandchildren know they can count on me to be there and to be supportive. And I do it in style. Kenette gets a kick out of all the bling I wear. She thinks I wear so much of it that it can be seen from space! She still calls it the "Mr. T Starter Kit." I have asked them if I can yell for them in support, and they said, "Yes, it's okay, as long as you yell for the other kids too!" I enjoy being a supporter of them all.

Life Principle: Involvement in Your Children's Lives
Demonstrates Your Love for Them

❖   I know that many mothers work full-time and cannot attend the afternoon activities of their children. If this is you, what evening or weekend activities can you attend?

❖   Is there a balance between outside activities for your children and having quiet time for the family? If not, how can you balance this out? What activities might need to be eliminated?

❖ Are your children involved in these activities because they want to be, or are you pushing your desires onto them? You might have to ask them.

❖ Do your words of support for your children show up in the actions you take?

In the verse below, James talks about faith needing works to be complete. I believe our love also needs works for it to be complete.

Thus also faith by itself, if it does not have works, is dead.... Do you see that faith was working together with his works, and by works faith was made perfect? –James 2:17, 22

Teaching Children Biblical Principles

In addition to being involved in our children's activities, we must intentionally put the Word before them consistently. Children usually want to play and have fun, and reading the Bible is not seen as being "fun" to them. But we can change that.

To motivate them, first, have a translation of the Bible that is easy for the children to understand. Second, get them involved in the actual reading of it. Ask them if there is a topic they want to learn more about. Then find the Scriptures for them (if they're too young to do the searching) that apply to that topic. Third, you can relate how their every day activities or goals for their future connect with Scriptures. Start this as soon as they are able to talk.

Our children learned many biblical principles from our family devotions. Some people may say, "That's just too hard to do," or "Dad isn't around." Pick a time when you can be together as a family *every day*. Simply read the Word for a while and have a short devotion—discussing how those Scriptures can apply to each of your lives. Then keep the Bible on the table as a visual reminder to everyone throughout the day.

When our kids started to read themselves, we let them pick the passages they wanted to read. I remember when one of the kids said, "I'm going to read today, 'Jesus wept.'" She apparently did not want to read too long, and we all laughed. Then we talked about how Jesus has the same feelings that we have. We made it into a mini devotional and then we all prayed. I also discovered that as we would pray "around", our kids could learn to pray at a very early age. We teach them how to do pray, not just at night before they go to bed, but also while around the table. They would say short prayers. Sometimes they got bored and I could tell they didn't want to pray, but teaching them spiritual principles day-by-day helped me to be the mother that God wanted me to be.

Are we also instructed to teach other children also? I think charity first begins at home. I think its fine to teach others. I taught Sunday school, which was a privilege. I sang in the choir, and I had to work. However, I trust that I never neglected my children. Start at home and then include your children's friends. Sometimes when friends would come to dinner, and we would ask them to pray. It may have been awkward for them, but I believe it also made a big impression.

One of the biggest lessons we can teach our children is the big picture of how the Word fits into our lives. There are reasons behind the do's and don'ts of Scripture. Everyone wants to have success in life yet many don't know how to obtain it. It's not dependent upon only our experience and talents. God plays a big role in it too. All throughout the Word there are examples of people who obey and follow God and they get blessed.

Life Principle: Planting the Seeds of God's Word
in Children brings Good Fruit

❖   Are you currently spending time in the Word and prayer daily with your children?

- ❖ If not, when is a good time of the day for you to begin? You may need to "make" time. If you don't know how to begin, pick up "The Daily Bread" or another daily devotional and begin by reading the Scripture for that day (read it out of the Bible so your children get used to seeing you use the Bible). Then read the blurb in the booklet. Now interact with your children to see how that verse can apply to their lives (and to your life).

- ❖ In the evening you can also do the "peak and pit" exercise mentioned earlier in this book. If your children are old enough, share your own peak and pit experience for the day.

This Book of the Law shall not depart from your mouth, but you shall meditate in it day and night, that you may observe to do according to all that is written in it. For then you will make your way prosperous, and then you will have good success. –Joshua 1:8

Acknowledging Your Children's Gifts

While your children are growing up, you teach them all the same principles, but as time goes on, you recognize their giftings. We sent Kenton to a club that taught him how to preach at an early age. We never said, "God called you to be a preacher." God had to call him, not us. We tried to put him in a place where he could best be schooled in the area that he was called to.

With my granddaughter, Holiday, I gave her tap dancing lessons. That wasn't for her. I gave her ballet dancing lessons. That wasn't for her. She was good in sports. So then we got her a track coach, she developed her talents, and it paid her way through school.

Encourage the gifts they choose, not the ones you choose. Many husbands, particularly ones that didn't participate in a sport, want their sons to be good in a sport. Some women are the same way. They want their daughter to pursue what they missed out on in life. Don't push them toward your bent, but direct them in their bent. Consider their strengths and let them tell you what they like.

When my children were still very young, I began to pray that God would guide them into the knowledge of what His will is for them. Also, that God would show me so I could encourage my children to pursue their God-given gifts and talents.

Since Doc and I have been in ministry for our entire marriage, we could share the wisdom and insights we learned along the road. We hope this saved them from discovering some hard lessons on their own. However, there are still lessons that could only be learned by going through the struggles.

I told my children how much God loved them and how He had a great plan for them. Then we sought out what those plans were for each of them. The search begins with understanding what each child's gifts are. Remember, if we ask God to guide us, He will. We weren't focused on what God didn't want them to do; rather, we focused on what God wanted to do in the positive. How could God use each child to carry out His vision for their life?

Life Principle: Look at the Gifts God has Given Your Child to Discern His or Her Calling in Life

---

❖ Do you know what spiritual gifts and natural talents your child has?

❖ If not, how does your child spend his or her time? What does he or she talk about all the time? There are also tests for spiritual gifts on the market to help guide you and your child.

❖ Do you see yourself imposing your desires on your child's

future? For each activity your child is involved in, ask if he or she wants to do it. Perhaps together you can find an activity your child will excel at.

For I know the thoughts that I think toward you, says the LORD, thoughts of peace and not of evil, to give you a future and a hope. –Jeremiah 29:11

Being a Working Mom

As I said before, I worked mainly because it was necessary to make money. I started as a secretary at a mortuary and I ended up running the business because I worked hard. It was difficult at times to manage work and my family, but I worked because it was a necessity.

I didn't work because I had an ambition to accomplish a goal. I did my job daily, and I accomplished a lot. I wasn't trying to buy material possessions, but to provide for what we needed.

I think it is ideal if a mother doesn't have to work. When the kids were finally all in school, it was necessary that I work. However, when they were young, I was home all the time. In their early years, we impart many values that our children will keep. During those first seven years, we influence their hearts and minds indelibly. Their actions, what they do, and how they think are formed in these early stages.

When it was necessary for me to work, I did. However, my family was always my priority. My job never took precedence. I made sure that even if I worked on the days when my children had activities, I would replace myself so I could go to my kid's games after school. My children were my passion.

The financial needs of today's families are different from when Doc and I were raising our children. Today's parents need to sit down and decide what their priorities are and what they have to have in order to meet the budget they have set for their family. Many times we mistake our wants for our needs. It is important to differentiate between our wants and our needs.

We met the need of providing for our children adequately. We sent all of our kids to college, and we paid for their education. That was one reason why I worked. Kandi went to USC, which was not inexpensive. However, when she attended, she still had to obey certain rules because we were paying the bill.

Once I was picked up to go to a function at USC by a mother in her Rolls-Royce. While we were traveling, she said, "I understand that you are still setting rules for your daughter. She is at school so she should be able to make her own decisions." I said, "I don't quite feel that way. Since I am furnishing the car, the gas, the clothes, and the tuition, I have something to say about the rules. If she does not obey the rules, then she can send herself through school." We stuck by our standards.

Life Principle: A Woman's Work When Ordained by God Produces Much Fruit

---

❖ Have you and your husband sat down and created a budget so you know where your money is being spent? Make plans to set aside some for emergencies, large purchases, and your children's education.

❖ Are you working because you're bored? Or because you want extra money to buy lavish things? To make ends meet? Because of peer pressure or pressure from your husband? Are you more career-focused than family-focused?

❖ Are you working at the expense of neglecting your children? You can work and balance your life with your husband and children, but be careful that you don't slowly get sucked into working more and more, especially long term.

Charm is deceitful and beauty is passing, but a woman who fears the LORD, she shall be praised.

Give her of the fruit of her hands, and let her own works praise her in the gates. – Proverbs 31:30-31

Living Beyond "Survival Mode"

Young moms have it tough these days. They can get pulled in so many different directions at one time. Soon they feel overwhelmed. It's like they're in survival mode all the time. Sometimes that's all they can do!

We had three children, and we didn't have any help in rearing them. Neither my folks nor my in-laws were around to help. Sometimes it is overwhelming, especially waking up after you've been up during the night because the kids were sick or had bad dreams. You're tired, they're not well, and making it through the day and doing the things you need to, getting them soup, or waiting on them—sometimes that's all we can do. Even a day like that is the day that God has made. We shouldn't feel guilty about being in survival mode. The devil is the one who gives us guilt. When we are good moms, and we are called to be that day-in and day-out, we do feel overwhelmed at times. But we shouldn't feel guilty or that we haven't done what God wanted us to do.

Sometimes, I did things that I didn't have the heart to tell my kids! It became a pattern, unknown to me, that whenever I ran over our cat, I bought them new shoes. After a while when the kids got new shoes, they became suspicious!

When a mom is working full time, attending her kids' activities, and fixing dinner for the family, finding time to relax can be difficult. Without being intentional to balance life, it is easy to slip into survival mode. Stress continues to build until everything feels out of control.

One of my jobs was as a Professor of Hermeneutics at a Bible College. I thoroughly enjoyed that job. Like most of the jobs I had, I kept my priorities in mind. That lifelong habit kept me out of trouble, and it kept me in God's will. It provided purpose for my life. I knew I wasn't doing things just to be doing them, but I was doing what God asked me to do as the wife and mother He wanted me to be.

Whenever I felt confused, I remembered that God is not the author of confusion. I looked at what I was trying to do in my own strength, in my own way, and in my own timing. Sometimes that wasn't God's way and that's why things felt out of place. So I would look at my time and activities and evaluate if my priorities were out of order.

Finances can be a major problem that causes a woman to feel like she's living in survival mode. It's not always overspending. Sometimes its not knowing what your income and expenses are on a monthly basis. The practical plan to get out of this state of confusion is to write down what your income and expenses are so you know where you stand. Once you establish what your bare minimum expenses are, then you will know how much money you have that can be used for other items.

The Word says to turn all our anxieties over to the Lord. How do I do that? I start by praying to God about my situation. Then I sit and wait to hear from the Lord. As I do this, my heart and mind get quiet. Then I read the Bible. The book of Psalms expresses some of my concerns and my emotional turmoil. Since the Word is alive, it speaks to me and helps me see my life and situation from God's perspective. Only after I get His perspective do I find the wisdom to know how to relieve the stress in my life. God always comes through and shows me His way.

Life Principle: Giving Your Anxieties to God
Brings God's Peace

❖ Do you go through times where you feel like you're living in "survival mode?" What is usually going on in your life at that time?

❖ Which area seems to regularly give you stress: your finances, your or your kids' overly busy schedule, your lack of knowing what your priorities are for your life, your anger toward a person or toward yourself, your frustration because you think you should be at a better place in life than where you are right now, your health, or your feeling of being stuck in some situation and not seeing the way out?

❖ If you are married, sit down with your husband and share your answers to the above two questions. Encourage him to look at his life and your marriage, and have him answer the questions. Then discuss how you can change things. What specific steps can you take? When will you start?

Search me, O God, and know my heart; Try me, and know my anxieties; And see if there is any wicked way in me, And lead me in the way everlasting. –Psalm 139:23-24

EIGHT

Handle Trials
God's Way

One of the greatest difficulties of our life was when Mark was born, and we learned he had Spina Bifida. He was six months old when he died. Although it was devastating, we did not stay in a state of depression.

The key reason I was able to maintain the proper perspective was because I had a husband who was supportive. One of the statements Doc made at the funeral was God never takes us through deep waters to drown us, only to cleanse us. I felt I had some lessons to learn because I had a comparatively easy life in my childhood and with my parents. I asked the Lord to teach me the lessons He wanted me to learn during that time and also to be a blessing to others.

When Mark was born, the doctor said, "Should we tell her, or should we wait?" Ken said, "She's a strong woman, you can tell her what the situation is." Because I had been memorizing Scripture, it was already inside me and the verse that came to mind was from Job 1:21, *the Lord gave, and the Lord has taken away; blessed be the name of the Lord."* That was my first thought when I heard that Mark wasn't going to live.

We saturated ourselves with Scripture. During difficult times, God brings His Word to our hearts and minds, and He teaches us. We learned many lessons about faith and trust, and we were able to bless many people through our lives.

I remember a woman in our church who had lost a child. She would not speak to anyone after the death of her baby. She would not eat and she cried all the time. She became suicidal and had to stay in the hospital. Her husband was distraught. He and the hospital chaplain did not know what to do with her. Her husband called me, and I was able to talk to her. Even though she would not even look at me, she would only face the wall, she listened when I told her, "I know exactly how you feel. My baby was taken from me too. I know you feel guilty and that maybe this was your fault, but it isn't! I understand how you feel." I told her, "You have two choices right now: whether you and your husband draw closer together or whether you are going to continue doing what you're doing right now, drawing away from him and drawing away from everyone who loves you and cares for you. I want to tell you that that's not going to help."

After that I was the only person she wanted to see. Day after day, I talked with her and told her she could make it. I told her God was with her. She finally understood and began eating. She saw hope that she could go on. She accepted Jesus as her Lord and Savior. Later she became pregnant again and went on to have four healthy children.

Years later God gave me other children and I praise Him for that. When something dramatic happens, becoming bitter is destructive. It doesn't help you get better. We need to recognize that God sends trials for a purpose. I can tell you that it's difficult. I'm not saying that you won't have a heavy heart. You will. My heart was very heavy after Mark's death. I had waited five years to have children. So for five years I wanted a child and God sent us Mark. But He only let us keep him for six months.

To this day when the phone rings at 2:00 or 3:00 in the morning, I jolt awake and think of Mark because he was in the hospital most of the time. A loss like that never completely leaves you, but you can have the peace of God that He promises to get you through difficult situations.

Would I choose to go through it again? No. I'm not that spiritual. But I have been able to be a blessing to others and have learned to trust Him, and that's how God uses our trials.

Physical Loss of a Loved One isn't the End

When you lose someone you love, you're not really losing them. If they know the Lord or if they're a young child under the age of accountability, they will be in heaven with you forever. Since I don't know how many more years I have left to serve the Lord, I take joy in looking forward to meeting Mark in heaven and I know he will be there.

My children ask me sometimes why I don't talk more about Mark. The reason I don't is because in Minneapolis, Minnesota, we had a lady in our church who never ever quite forgave God for taking her first son away. She would throw this up to her daughters and saying, "Why did God do this, and why aren't you like your brother?" I made up my mind I wasn't going to do that. I would talk about it whenever they wanted to. I would be a blessing to others when given the chance. However, I didn't want to live in the past. I knew

God had given me more children and I was going to be the best mother I could be to them.

Blaming God doesn't help, but having faith that He never takes us through deep waters to drown us, but to cleanse us and to teach us lessons on how to be a blessing, perhaps not to ourselves, but to others.

Life Principle: Being Victorious in Trials
                   Brings Comfort and Hope to Others

❖ Are you stuck in a hurt from your past? Are you blaming God for it? If so, will you let God off the hook and move on with your life?

❖ If another person hurt you, have you forgiven that person? Remember, once you forgive you should not bring up that hurt again.

❖ Have you been able to use your trials and victories to help other people? If not, ask God to guide you to people who you can help.

❖ Do you find yourself repeatedly talking about your hurtful past? Or are you using it as an excuse for your thoughts and behavior today? When those memories come up, how can you turn your thoughts toward God instead of rehashing your hurt?

❖ If you have lost a loved one who was a Christian or a small child (even unborn), can you take hope in the fact that you *will* see that person in heaven and be together for eternity?

Blessed be the God and Father of our Lord Jesus Christ, the Father of mercies and God of all comfort, who comforts us in all our tribulation, that we may be able to comfort those who are in any trouble, with the comfort with which we ourselves are comforted by God. –II Corinthians 1:3-4

Some Trials are Self-Made

Not all of our trials come from unexpected tragedies. As I've mentioned throughout this book, when we do things our way instead of God's way, we bring unnecessary anxieties and trials upon ourselves. Self-centered attitudes and behaviors can cause others to react negatively toward us. We may wonder why they're acting that way and not realize that something we did or said caused them to respond that way.

Sometimes we feel like we are in a downward spiral that we can't escape. We feel trapped like a bug in a spider's web. At that point we need to cry out to the Lord like David did in Psalm 25:15-17:

> *My eyes are ever toward the LORD, For He shall pluck my feet out of the net. Turn Yourself to me, and have mercy on me, For I am desolate and afflicted. The troubles of my heart have enlarged; Bring me out of my distresses!*

There is *always* a way out of our trials, no matter who brought them about. Once we have passed a trial, we shouldn't let it go to waste. Ask God to show you how you can use it to help others who may be going through the same type of trial.

I think about positive things, even through difficult times. I focus by asking, *Lord, what do You want me to learn through these tough times?* It doesn't mean I didn't hurt or that it wasn't hard, nor am I saying everything was always a bed of roses. It wasn't. But I would bring the situation to mind and start thinking and quoting Scripture and singing praises to God. I'd keep my mind in a mode of praise and thanksgiving so that I wouldn't go down a negative road. Once you start being bitter, you do not become better. You only become more bitter. It's like taking poison and expecting somebody else to reap the results. When we have bitterness in our hearts, it's poison. We can help ourselves by clearing our minds, and through faith, focusing on forgiveness and gratitude. The devil wants us to stay stuck in our bitterness.

For instance, I had just had my 85th birthday party, and for the first Sunday in weeks, I was feeling good. Then I fell and broke my arm in two places. Shortly after that, we were in Palm Springs, and I found myself feeling sorry for myself. I thought, *This isn't right.* I told myself, *Lois, don't go down that road!* So even after you've been a Christian for many years, you can still start down that road. You need to put the stop sign up immediately. Don't even let the yellow light stay on. Instead, thank God and say, "I don't understand it." Would I choose to go through it? No way. Does it hurt? Yes. Do I want it? No. But, it's here for a purpose, so I've got to do the best I can with it and not complain and not be bitter.

Life Principle: Glory in Your Tribulations
For They Produce Perseverance

❖ What's your first reaction to trials? Anger? Resentment? Having a pity party? To lash out at others? To internalize it? To withdraw from others? To blame others? To blame God?

❖ OR, do you praise God and thank Him and have faith that He will sustain you and guide you through the trial successfully?

❖ Have you noticed that some of your trials seem to be focused around the same type of issue?

Perhaps you haven't learned the lesson that God wants to teach you? Write down what you think those issues are and ask God to help you learn the lesson and not walk away from them.

❖ To "glory in your tribulation" means to give God worshipful praise, honor, and thanksgiving, not necessarily for the trial itself, but for how it will change you as you go through it and for how God will be glorified for getting you through it.

Therefore, having been justified by faith, we have peace with God through our Lord Jesus Christ, through whom also we have access by faith into this grace in which we stand, and rejoice in hope of the glory of God. And not only that, but we also glory in tribulations, knowing that tribulation produces perseverance; and perseverance, character; and character, hope. Now hope does not disappoint, because the love of God has been poured out in our hearts by the Holy Spirit who was given to us. –Romans 1-5

A table filled with memories at my 85th birthday party.

NINE

A Virtuous Wife
and Mother

The woman described in Proverbs 31:10-31 seems almost like a fairy tale —too good to be true yet we must understand that nothing is impossible when God leads and guides us. Is the virtuous wife and mother described in the proverb perfect? No! No one is perfect except Jesus Christ.

Let's consider how we can become like this woman of faith. God can and will use you today, no matter what your past has been like.

In preparing to write this book, each of my family members was asked for their input on how their lives were influenced by my life as their wife and mother. These are not shared out of pride, but as an example of how God can use an imperfect lady, who loves Him and obeys Him, to build a godly life that affects not only her family, but everyone she comes into contact with.

Doc

Lois made me feel that I could do anything. It meant everything to me that Lois encouraged me so much. She helped me realize that I could preach and move people with my ministry. She was not critical, but positive in every area. She made me feel that I was ten feet tall and the smartest guy in the world. She's smarter than I am, but never let me know that.

When I started out in the ministry, a traveling evangelist came to our school. He had recently had a baby boy, and to those of us who were preparing to preach, he said, "Men, I held that little boy up to God and said if he comes between You and my ministry, then take that boy home." I had a chill go through me when I realized that his ministry should be to his son first, not his ministry to others. I knew the Bible says that if any does not take care of his own family, he has denied the faith.

So I understood that my kids and my wife came first. Lois was wise enough that when I was away at a meeting, she would keep up with the Scripture reading with the children. Then when I came home we would have a special time to make up for the time I was gone. But I was in itinerant Bible teacher for two and a half years, and I realized I couldn't be a good father and be gone so much. One year I made five trips across the county because many of the Bible conferences were back East. I finally went back into the pastorate so I could spend more time with my kids.

When I was growing up, we used to have evangelists come to the church and they would say, "Pray for my son, he's going to hell." And I thought, *preachers have kids that go to hell?* When I was a little kid of only eight years old, I knew I was called to preach. I said, "God, I want to make a deal with You. If I give You my life to be a minister, I want You to give me my kids." God gave me a very wise wife and wisdom beyond what I had to help me be the father that I ought to.

94

One time in the morning when I was going to leave Lois and the kids and go to church, Kenette said, "Don't leave, Daddy." And I wanted to say, "Well, daddy's got to go save souls and do something spiritual." But instead I heard myself saying, "Kenette, daddy has to go to work. Your little girlfriend Mary's daddy goes to work. Martha's daddy goes to work. Daddies go to work. And I go to work to make money so I can buy you a bicycle." She said, "Okay, Daddy, go to work." I didn't make the church a calling to my kids. I made it my normal work. It was something that I did to support the family, and they understood that. I never wanted the church taking their daddy from the kids. I think preacher's kids often resent that. My kids always came first.

Part of Lois' ability to encourage was that she set dates for birthdays, even before we had kids. We spent time affirming each other. Lois was very wise in giving affirmation. She knows how to satisfy me in food, sexually, and every way imaginable, and she studied these things, which a wise wife will do, and not seek her own. The Bible makes it clear that a husband's body doesn't belong to him, and the wife's body doesn't belong to her. They belong to each other. Dr. Wheat's book, *Intended for Pleasure* is a book that every married couple should read together. Lois made our marriage happy in every area.

Lois was sacrificial for her kids. She did things for them before she would do them for herself. She was selfless in making sure that the kids had what they needed before she sought her own needs. The kids greatly appreciated that. As a preacher, I never made over $28,000 a year, so we had to be very careful with our funds. Lois knew how to make funds stretch. When we shopped, we always went down to the wholesale areas in Los Angeles. She knows how to buy food. I would take the paper off and I would say, "What should the price be?" I had the prices advertised. She would know the prices there. She'd make friends with the butcher to know how to get the best cuts, so we could have things that other families couldn't afford.

We created activities that didn't cost a lot of money. We went on picnics. She thought about ways to have fun that were exciting yet without being costly. Today, parents think that kids have got to go to Disneyland. I think our kids had as much fun doing the events that we planned. We would go down to the river. We didn't even have a tent. We'd just put sleeping bags on the shore. At times we would go with a friend who had a boat. We taught our kids to water ski at early ages. We'd make it the way the settlers did in the country and the kids thought that was great—sleeping under the stars without a tent.

Our parents were very strict, and we were raised in a very strict part of the country. When we joined a church, we had to sign that we wouldn't drink, dance, smoke, play cards, or go to movies. Because of this, we didn't let our first kid go to dances or to movies. We were probably beyond strictness. However, Lois was wise enough to ease up on many things before I was. She brought balance, but the kids knew that they had strict boundaries.

For instance, Kenton wanted a very high-powered car. When he was about 17 or 18, he could buy it himself when he made enough money working in our cemetery. I looked at that Camaro with the hopped-up engine in it, traction master big tires in the back, and I said, "Kenton, can you handle it?" He said, "I can handle it, Dad." I said, "Let's make an agreement. How many tickets before you get rid of it?" I was willing to go two. He said, "Dad, if I get one, I'll give it up." He never got a ticket. I drove it twice and got stopped by the cops each time!

We set boundaries like that and the kids knew that we would stand on their side. Lois told our kids, "You'll be pressured to do things you shouldn't do. If you don't want to take the pressure yourself, say 'my parents won't let me do that.' Call us up and make it as though we're saying no." One day Kenette called asking if she could go somewhere. It sounded all right to me. Then I heard her say, "Well Dad, you're terrible! You don't let me do anything!" She started railing at me. I knew what she was doing. It took the pressure off of her so she didn't have to make that decision. She said "My dad and mom are so strict. They'll kill me if I do that."

We also kept our kids in church in good youth departments. Our son-in-law, Gene, was our youth director. Kenton became the youth director in our church. Having kids in ministry and doing ministry at early ages was very important.

My most memorable event with Lolo was our honeymoon! We have had wonderful times together. We would generally take our vacations where we would go to a Bible conference, and then we would get away together. Those were always wonderful times.

I think one of the most memorable events was the tragedy of our first-born who lived for six months and then died. That was a hard time. But to see Lois' strength through that and to see how she clung to the Lord during that time and looked to me for strength, I realized I had to be there to give her strength. I think that was foundational in our lives where we gave our strength to each other, which we found from the Lord. That gave us solidarity in our marriage at a very early time.

Lois always set the Bible when she set the table. We read Scripture every night and set Scriptural principles before the kids. For instance, on Sundays, we always had a great dinner that Lois would prepare. I built a round table with a Lazy Susan in the middle so we didn't have to pass food, and at a round table, you can see each other. Then Lois would invite the kids' friends to come over for dinner so we could meet them. We would tell our kids to invite their friends. The kids realized later on in life, more than maybe we did, that we were trying to get them to choose certain friends over others. When we met with the kids, we'd say, why don't you invite them to go along with us or have dinner with us? Lois skillfully welcomed the friends to our home.

Then we would pray, and our kids would pray in front of their friends, and we'd say to them, "We have devotions together, and you can sit there and listen, but each of us has a short prayer, so just realize that." Then we'd position our kids in front of their friends that way. Lois did that so that the kids didn't really realize that we were helping pick their friends for them. I think that was one of the great strengths of our family—having that Sunday dinner was a marvelous time at our round table and inviting friends to be part of it.

What is Lois' number one character trait? I always laughingly say she's lived with me for 66 years, and I haven't corrupted her. She is incorruptible. I've never heard her use a swear word. She has held such a high standard all through her life. That's amazing, particularly living with a guy like me who is very corruptible!

Kenette

What is the most memorable event with your mom?

My mom led me to the Lord when I was five years old, and I can remember it like it was yesterday. Every night before I went to sleep, we had this ritual. I would lie down on my bed half way under the covers, and she would tickle my back, and she would pray with me. That particular night she prayed that I would be a lover of Jesus, and that I would come to know Him and be His child. Then she asked the Lord to protect me. When I heard her prayers that night, I started asking questions about heaven and what it meant to be a child of God. I told her I wanted to be a lover of Jesus, and she explained to me what it meant to be a child of God. Then she had me pray the prayer of salvation. After I prayed, she told me there was a party going on in heaven for ME! She began explaining all about the party that the angels and Jesus were having. We had a blast visualizing that event together. I will never forget that night as long as I live.

What actions or influence that your mom had on you while you were growing up are you intentionally trying to do with your own children or grandchildren?

Every morning I woke up and saw my mom on her knees reading her Bible. She always gave us the verse, "This is the day that the Lord hath made, rejoice and be glad in it" to wake us up. We always saw her having her time with the Lord. So that value was instilled in me. My mom is a strong woman who not only mentored her own children, but others. Everywhere I go people tell me, "Your mom took me to lunch. She's praying for me." They tell me how God has answered their prayers because of her prayers for them. I think seeing her in the Word and praying every day with her has been the greatest influence on me that I want to carry on with my children and grandchildren.

99

Mom helped me raise my kids. I went back to get my Masters in Marriage and Family Counseling, and I became an educator. Mom took care of my kids every Tuesday and Thursday night. They played tennis and had so much fun. My kids loved it. She made dinner for them and they prayed together. My dad led the devotions at dinner. Mom helped me while I went to school for those three years getting my Masters degree. She has always been an unbelievable influence on my kids.

Growing up we always had a family devotion that my dad would lead. My husband and I tried to do the same for our children at dinner. During those three years when I was getting my degree, she kept this wonderful time of devotion with my children. She has always been an unbelievable influence on my kids. They know how much she prays for them, and they have always known how much they were loved and cared for by my parents. Even now, my kids bowl with them every week. The grandkids are able to go during the summer. They take off on Fridays when they can to bowl with them because they love them so much. They all have bowling shirts that have "Papa's Holy Rollers" embroidered on the back. It is precious to see their love and devotion to them.

How did your mom influence your friends?

Our house was always open to anybody. She always had extra food even when we did not have much money. I always tell the joke of how we ate communion for breakfast, lunch, and dinner, but somehow mom always made extra of whatever we were having and made it so delicious. I could always invite my friends over any time. One of my girlfriends, whose dad was an alcoholic, actually lived with us for a while. We always had people in our home that lived with us for a while if they needed help. Our doors were always open. My parents witnessed by their lives and by loving my friends. I appreciate their welcoming approach to people.

What are two of the most important life lessons?

I think prayer and being in the Word every day. Even now while I'm on my way to work, I'll call mom and we pray together. We mark off all the prayer requests that God has answered. So we pray every morning before we go to work. In fact, her life of prayer influenced me to write a short booklet on it. It's in Appendix A.

What was the greatest way your mom influenced your spiritual growth?

I remember living in a parsonage ("parsonage" is Christianese for tenement living). We were so poor, but mom, always bold with her faith, constantly requested God to provide for us. So we got to watch how God provided. Growing up, Mom always sang, and she played the piano. She was genuinely happy. She never complained that the Sunday school classes were held in our house, and she felt I shouldn't complain either when the nursery was in my bedroom. When I complained about the dirty diaper smell when I got my room back after church on Sundays, she took me to a church member's home and showed me that her children didn't have their own rooms and that the whole family lived in two rooms. After that day I never complained about the dirty diaper smell. Mom worked hard to teach us to be grateful. She modeled her gratitude and helped us grow up without bitterness toward the church.

Even now the number of people that she touches is amazing to me, and now it is her turn to let others be a blessing to her. Although it is hard for her to let other people help her because she has been accustomed to being the giver, she is slowly allowing people to help her. She has macular degeneration which is attacking her eyes, and since her knee replacement and two broken shoulders, she cannot drive. When she was told that she couldn't drive, it was very hard on her. She felt like she had lost her independence and that she would be a burden to have people pick her up and take her on errands. She also has let other people take on her duties that she has been so faithful with. Mom, to her great surprise, has learned that people love to pick her up. They still want to take her to lunch and have her pray for them.

Mom is aging so gracefully, and she never complains about her eyesight or the pain in her shoulders or knee. When I can tell she is in pain or saddened by not being able to see, I say, "Mom, I'm so sad for you," and she always responds with, "Kenette, I am so very blessed I have had such wonderful health my whole life, I cannot complain now for this blindness or these old joints. I am so very fortunate." I hope she can teach me to age more gracefully.

Out of all the children and grandchildren of Lolo, there are seven pastors who are serving the Lord, and the rest are bringing up their families in the church and trying their best to live in a way pleasing to the Lord. This is a huge legacy.

Many of my friends have been in ministry. I know pastors' kids from way back, and they're bitter with God and their families, and they will have nothing to do with the church. Mom always loved serving the Lord, and considered it a great calling. She was never bitter, and she never put her ministry before her husband or her children. Mom lived as though she knew that God had called her to be a wife, mom, and grandmother first, and she was always our biggest fan and our LOUDEST cheerleader.

Kenton, Jr.

What is the most memorable event with your mom?

I have many wonderful memories of my mom. When I played sports growing up, Mom came to my games and she would scream, and she was loud. Her presence was felt. She was always "so there" for me as her kid. It's just as true now for her grandkids. She is overwhelmingly there for you. She yells and is excited, which at times was overwhelming, but at the same time was reassuring.

As a teenager, at first it was a little awkward because I felt a sense of embarrassment. But watching my friends, I realized they looked at it and thought, "I wish my mom was that willing to be so out there for me and to be crazy and bold and screaming encouragement and affirmation." It's one of the defining things I remember as a kid.

My mom is the more athletic of my parents. My dad has a couple of sports he's interested in. He bowls and his focus on athletics came from his father. But my mom was more athletic. I remember as a little kid, I wanted to learn how to play tennis. She'd say, "I'll play tennis with you," and she did. As I tried different sports, she would jump in and try to be involved.

What actions or influence did your mom have on you while you were growing up that you are intentionally trying to do with your own children?

My mom is very affirming. She's the one who started a family tradition that at birthdays we affirm each other. My mom made that a priority as we were growing up. She would have us answer the question, "What is it that you love about (the person's name)?" She created an affirming environment, and all of us have followed her with this same kind of support in our families.

She is not Pollyanna; she is a truly optimistic person. In any situation, she finds a positive way to look at it. I can remember my mom reframing situations that as a kid I'd think, "This is terrible, or this didn't go right, or it didn't happen the way that it should." She would, but in a very real way, say, "Yes, but look, we have this opportunity to do this." So she is a "see the silver lining in a cloud" type of person. She has pulled it off authentically through her whole life.

She's a person of faith. She prays. I watched her in the mornings when I would get up, and she would be praying for us. She marked our whole family by being a model of prayer.

How are your mom (and dad) an influence on your children in actions and words?

As grandparents and at their age, we all are absolutely amazed at the impact they have on our kids. My sons are all over 25 now, and she and my dad bowl with them every Friday. What's wonderful is that at their age, they want to. That's been going on for a number of years. Right now, my parents are surprisingly very close. My parents make it a priority to be there every week and rarely miss one. My kids orchestrate their lives around the Friday lunch hour bowling times. They have this delightful relationship with them where they laugh and play together. It's something my dad can do; in fact, he's actually pretty good at it. He knows what he's talking about, and he likes to be in that environment. They pay for it, and then they take them to lunch. I'm amazed at the impact they're having on my kids. At their age, my parents could choose not to be around their grandkids. But they understand how valuable it is to stay connected, and they do it intentionally. They model a loving marriage for my sons. They love and pray for their grandkids and great grandkids. This time invested has had a great reward...their grandkids listen to them.

How did your mom influence your friends as you were growing up?

My mom was very intentional. It was obvious she wanted to know who my friends were. The way she expressed it was to choose to be the home where there was food, and everyone was always welcome. If any of my friends showed up, she'd say, "Hey, do you want something to eat?" or "Can you stay for dinner?" She made our family dinnertime a place where friends were invited. She intentionally pursued them. None of them would choose to establish a relationship with my parents—you know high school kids don't necessarily want a relationship with parents—but she valued them. My friends had great relationships with my parents. My mom wanted to have a relationship with them, and this gave her a voice in their lives.

How did that affect you and your relationship with your friends?

My friends wanted to be at my house. My mom was always making something good to eat. It was a place of hospitality. As a result, they came to my house more than I went to theirs. Friends are different on a spectrum of being a little bit more prone to trouble or a little less prone to trouble. She was gentle and kind and knew that "birds of a feather flock together." When I was around someone that was a little bit more prone to trouble, she wouldn't ever say anything bad about them, but instead she always talked about the friends that she thought were heading more in the right direction.

We obviously went to church. She boldly invited all my friends to church. That was startling as a kid. I don't think I would have done that. But then they got to see our life of faith, and they were invited into that. She was bold in that way.

What are the two most important life lessons your mom taught you?

My mom has lived a courageous life of faith in front of me. Our life as a family did not proceed in a straight line. In some of the darkest moments we went through, my mom's faith shone the brightest. Prayer is what sustained her. She has a great love for God which is real, vibrant, and observable.

The power of a parent is to create a family atmosphere. She wanted to create the culture of our family, how we connected, how we spent time together, and she defined that. We told the truth to each other as a family. We were unified as a family. She created community.

We were a displaced family when we moved from Denver back to California. We didn't have any family relations in California. My dad was planting a church, and he was on the radio. My older sister and I were in junior high, and my younger sister was elementary school. We had nobody. My mom realized there needed to be an extended family. She knew about another family who they knew from their college days, a solid Christian family, and she saw them at church. My mom went to them and developed a relationship with them, and she literally said to them after a couple of weeks, "We have no family, will you be family for us?"

My parents didn't know how to go on vacation. So this family took us to the river for the first time, and we went water skiing with them. It became a family tradition which we did for the next 30 years. Ultimately, their daughter, Laurie, became my wife so that worked out great for me. Our families went through those high school years, which were treacherous, together. We made an extended family. There were things that my parents couldn't say to me—when you're in high school there are certain things you can't hear from your parents—but I could hear from Conky and Earl. I remember Conky saying, "Kenton, you shouldn't do that, people won't like you." It was startling! It was an abrasive way to be treated, and it shocked me, but I heard it, and I changed. Our two families had more fun together, camping and going to the river, and my parents would have never figured that out without this relationship.

What is the greatest way she influenced your spiritual growth?

She lived her faith, and she prayed. She taught my Sunday school at different times in my life. There isn't anything I remember her saying. It was what she did. More is caught than taught. Her biggest effect is what I caught over the years, not ever the words she said.

Kandis (Kandi)

What is your most memorable event with your mom?

Every event with my mom is memorable because in anything we do, she is our biggest cheerleader. She is always an enthusiastic part of all the family events and activities we are involved in, and she makes everything special for us.

My mom desires to see all of her grandchildren's weddings. Recently, my oldest son, Trevor, was married in Costa Rica. Of course, my mom did not hesitate to be part of the ceremony. She made all of our adventures more fun, including feeding alligators and kayaking!

What actions or influence that your mom had on you while you were growing up are you intentionally trying to do with your own children?

Every morning she woke up to pray and walk. She chose a block to walk where she prayed for each one of us. I think that is one of the actions that I remember that I also do for my own children. I also want to be consistent the way she is.

Mom was always so involved with us, our kids, our friends, and others. She called people all the time to tell them she was praying for them today. This had a big impact. My kids always knew they had a huge advocate behind them which made them feel very important.

How are your mom and dad influencing your children or grandchildren?

She lives with us so she has always been with my kids. We built a second story for my mom and dad so my mom and dad basically were there all the time for my kids. They saw how they worked, how they played, and how they invested in others. They also saw how others responded to them because they were their grandchildren.

Their balance and consistency were seen in all parts of their lives. My mom always asks my kids, "How can I pray for you guys?" That is significant for them. Their work in Africa made it possible for me to meet and adopt our fourth child, Taps, from Zimbabwe. My children were able to see how they serve God with joy.

How did your mom influence your friends as you were growing up? How does she influence your current friends?

Her influence is incredible because the way she lives her life is consistent with what she says and believes. Every day she gets up, puts her feet on the ground, and thinks what she can do for God. With that, people see how her words and actions line up, how she lives her life for God's work. That makes her very attractive to my friends. They want to learn from her and have her disciple them.

What are the most important life lessons your mom taught you?

She always put God first, she was very consistent, and she had fun every day. She thought of creative ways to make life fun. She didn't need to have a lot of money to create lasting memories for us when we were growing up. On weekends, we would go bowling and get pizza. It was important for her to make sure that she had us around. She always made us feel important.

What was the greatest way she influenced your spiritual growth?

She memorized Scripture and quoted it often. Philippians 4:8 was a verse which she wanted to impress on our hearts and minds. *"Whatever is true, whatever is honorable, whatever is just, whatever is pure, whatever is lovely, whatever is commendable, if there is any excellence, if there is anything worthy of praise, think about these things."*

My mom's greatest influence is the consistency of her spiritual walk. She wouldn't say, "Oh, I'm getting up in the morning, and I'm going to pray for you." She just did it. I saw how she lived. Instead of her telling me about it, she lived it out in front of me.

Living YOUR Legacy

Now it's your time to consider. What type of legacy are you leaving your family and friends?

What do you want to be remembered for?

I hope my memories and choices have helped you consider what you want to live for.

My hope is to be remembered as a woman who prayed for others, who loved the Lord with all her heart, and who laughed abundantly.

The Virtuous Wife

Who can find a virtuous wife?
For her worth is far above rubies.

The heart of her husband safely trusts her;
So he will have no lack of gain.

She does him good and not evil
All the days of her life.

She seeks wool and flax,
And willingly works with her hands.

She is like the merchant ships,
She brings her food from afar.

She also rises while it is yet night,
And provides food for her household,
And a portion for her maidservants.

She considers a field and buys it;
From her profits she plants a vineyard.

She girds herself with strength,
And strengthens her arms.

She perceives that her merchandise is good,
And her lamp does not go out by night.

She stretches out her hands to the distaff,
And her hand holds the spindle.

She extends her hand to the poor,
Yes, she reaches out her hands to the needy.

She is not afraid of snow for her household,
For all her household is clothed with scarlet.

She makes tapestry for herself;
Her clothing is fine linen and purple.

Her husband is known in the gates,
When he sits among the elders of the land.

She makes linen garments and sells them,
And supplies sashes for the merchants.

Strength and honor are her clothing;
She shall rejoice in time to come.

She opens her mouth with wisdom,
And on her tongue is the law of kindness.

She watches over the ways of her household,
And does not eat the bread of idleness.

Her children rise up and call her blessed;
Her husband also, and he praises her:

"Many daughters have done well,
But you excel them all."

Charm is deceitful and beauty is passing,
But a woman who fears the LORD, she shall be praised.

Give her of the fruit of her hands,
And let her own works praise her in the gates.

– Proverbs 31:10-31

ROCK of Africa Mission Outreach to Zimbabwe and Zambia, Africa

APPENDIX

APPENDIX

This poem was a wonderful gift on my 85th birthday
from my dear friend, Dale Sprowl.

You GLOW, Girl

by Dale Sprowl

Those who look to Him are radiant. Psalm 34:5

Lolo, you glow,
you light up a room like a chandelier, crystal and elegant,
reflecting light and creating color.

Like a candle, you soften us,
and like a fire, you warm and inspire us.

Your eyes, bright and blue, shine with smiles.
In your laughing and loving and living,
you lighten us,
brighten us with your light,
The Light,
Delight.

Lolo— you glow.

A Mother Who Prays
and a God Who Listens *by Kenette Molway*

B right with anticipation, three little sets of eyes would peer through the radiant beam of sunlight. Every morning they awoke to this vision, the wonder of their Mommy on her knees before the holy God in the brilliant rays of the sun—because their Mommy loved the mornings best.

Why the anticipation? Because those three little children knew what was coming. Like the faithful rising of the sun, Mommy's prayers lifted up to the Father every morning every single day. First she would seek the touch of God on her own life. She would beseech the Lord: "God, please create in me the person you want me to be; without You I am nothing. Please give me the wisdom and strength to be a good wife and mother." Next she would pray earnestly for her God-given mate. Then, as three little pairs of ears listened, she would present at the throne of Almighty God her priceless treasures, her children.

And God Always Listened

Finally, knowing as mothers somehow do that her little cherubs were eagerly watching and waiting, she would jump up and say, "Good morning! This is the day that the Lord has made! Rejoice and be glad in it!" With a swift hug for each giggling child, she would proclaim, "I love you!" and ask, "How can I pray for you today?" Eyes wide with sincerity, the three would ask, "Mommy, do your prayers do any good?" She would respond, "Do my prayers do any good? They most certainly do! That's why I pray and pray and pray, just for you."

Mommy's faith was strong and convincing, and by breakfast time the children would eagerly share their many requests. Then, assured that their needs were in good hands, they would skip off to play the day away while Mommy prayed.

114

And God Always Listened

As the seasons passed, the children grew and eventually went to school. Then Mommy began to pray by the block! Each precious child got one whole, long block, as Mommy walked before the Lord to intercede for her family. To the south was Kenton's block. Past the blue house and around the corner, and there was Kenette's block. Up the little hill and past the big oak tree, Mommy would begin to walk Kandi's block.

Mommy would pray, as promised, for things like caterpillars and the adopted bird with a broken wing, and for the monsters under the bed to go away. And, of course, there was the hamster that wasn't feeling very well, having failed his audition as an Indy-500 racecar. Step by dedicated step, Mommy would pray for angels to surround and protect each of them. As asked, she would pray for the kitties that ran away and for His healing of the puppy that couldn't fly after all. She would humbly ask God to give each of her children wisdom to make godly decisions, to choose good friends, and to live no wasted years.

She would ask God to keep each child in the palm of His almighty hand. Her work yet unfinished, Mommy would then add more blocks and pray for best friends and children she didn't even know yet, the future mates of her own children.

And God Always Listened

Faithful through the years, Mommy continued her vigil. Every day she would kneel before the Lord in the early morning, because Mommy loved mornings best. And she would greet her children with her cheerful quotation: "Good morning! This is the day that the Lord has made! Rejoice and be glad in it!" Then she would give them a loving squeeze and say, "I love you! How can I pray for you today?" Still her youngsters would ask, "Mommy, do your prayers do any good?" As always, Mommy would assure them, "They most certainly do! That's why I pray and pray and I pray, just for you."

As her children grew and matured, their prayer requests also grew and matured. Their breakfast-table requests had grown to include important matters like the changing of mean teachers into nice teachers, for good luck at musical recitals and games, for new bikes, and relief from playground bullies. Around the blocks Mommy would deliberately march, praying as she went.

And God Always Listened

In no time at all, the one-time toddlers became TEENAGERS! Greeted with their mother's morning rally in her perky and happy voice, "Good morning! This is the day that the Lord has made! Rejoice and be glad in it," they would tic and hiss, growl, and roll over, *begging* that she go away. Undaunted, Mommy, now "Mom," would declare, "I love you! How can I pray for you today?" Mom may have loved mornings best, but her teenagers did not! Sometimes they would toss pillows at her and plead, "Please, Mom, let us sleep. God isn't even up yet. This early in the morning your prayers can't possibly do any good!" Mom would respond with vigor, "God never sleeps, and He always listens. Of course my prayers do good; they most certainly do. That's why I pray and I pray and I pray just for you." Knowing that their Mom would not go away, the teens would sarcastically tell their Mom to pray for a new mother for them, one who would not wake them with such a perky and happy voice, asking them for prayer requests.

Still, Mom never stopped walking and praying. Not always certain how to handle three active, independent teens, she added more blocks to her prayer regimen. The neighborhood was hers, consecrated as a prayer path. She would intercede for them, as her adolescents encountered the unique pressures and turmoil of their generation. Sensing their need, she would spend even more hours on her knees in prayer for them. She wore out her knees seeking wisdom for herself and for her husband, and she fervently kept praying for her teenagers, even through hard times and poor choices.

And God Always Listened

By and by, the storms of the teen years were weathered, and the children went off to college. Still their Mom remained faithful in her morning prayers—because she loved mornings best. Her heart full of love, she would phone her children each week and remind them, "I love you! How can I pray for you today?" Since the faithful prayers of their godly mother had educated them, her young adults willingly shared their requests: "Mom, please pray for our classes and that we get good grades on our finals." They would ask prayer for special boyfriends and girlfriends. As their spiritual maturity began to unfold, each child would add, "Mom, please pray that God will keep me in the palm of His almighty hand. And, Mom, thanks; I love you too." Then, of course, their Mom would hang up the phone, to walk and pray.

And God Always Listened

Eventually, in answer to their mother's prayers, each child chose wisely in selecting a mate. One by one, as Mom met each fiancée for the first time, she would say, "So you're the one I've been praying for all these years!" And then God awarded her with a mother's most awesome miracle—grandchildren! When she met each new grandchild, she would say, "Hello, God's Little Gift. I'm going to pray for you every morning," because Mom, now "Grandma" loved mornings best.

Adding to her prayer blocks, she would present each blessed child to God for His safekeeping. When her grandchildren were old enough to talk, she would tell them, "I love you!" and ask, "How can I pray for you today?"

She then took each little toddler on a tour of his or her own special block, showing them where she walked and prayed just for that little soul. She prayed for wisdom and no wasted years for them. She always prayed that God would keep them in the palm of His almighty hand.

And God Always Listened

This Grandma never missed one of her grandchildren's games, track meets, recitals, or programs. She was their biggest fan and she always clapped and cheered the loudest. And even while she was cheering and clapping, Grandma was praying that each of her beloved grandchildren would always do his or her best.

And God Always Listened

As the years rolled by, the morning sun would always find Grandma on her knees before the Lord, praying for her children, who were now raising TEENAGERS of their own. Then, with her walking shoes on, ready to do battle, she would call her children one by one and say, "I love you! How can I pray for you today?" Now dedicated fans of their praying mother, each grown child would blurt out, "Oh, Mom, I was just on my knees praying for my kids. It's so hard to raise TEENAGERS! Do you think my prayers are doing any good? Please pray with me." And she would encourage her frazzled children, "You know by now all the good our prayers do. That's why I pray and pray and I pray just for you."

Then Grandma would set off to walk and pray. She had worn out her knees and nearly walked out a groove in the neighborhood pavement praying for her own children, but she kept on praying. She prayed that her teenaged grandchildren would have wisdom, make good friends, live no wasted years, and remain in the palm of His almighty hand.

And God Always Listened

Early in the morning, although it's been many years, Grandma still paces the blocks and prays. Whether the sun shines or the rain pelts, each darling grandchild can watch their grandma walking as they drive to school, and each one knows which is his or her block and can proudly say, "She's praying for me!"

Now, as I kneel in the warmth of the morning sun, I thank God that this amazing mother is my mother. Because of her, my brother and sister and I, with all our precious children, know that we are loved and prayed for.

And God Always Listened

Africa Heat, Dust, Exhaustion, Cramped Taxi – and Joy?

by V. Glen Megill

A s a member of the ROCK of Africa Mission Outreach Team in 2005, 80 year old Lolo Beshore was more than up to the task. The team kept a very rigorous schedule delivering relief supplies and Bibles to many rural villages in Zimbabwe, and all team members were hot and understandably exhausted as the team crossed the border into the country of Zambia.

With no ROCK of Africa Mission vehicles immediately available in Zambia, it was decided taxis should be used to reach the very rural village destination. However, with a team of six and many boxes of maize seed, mosquito nets, and Bibles, at least two taxis would be needed.

At the border crossing the team found only one taxi so they waited and waited – hot and very tired. After a forty minute wait *and* petitions of prayer, the ever optimistic and cheerful Lolo said, "Come on. All we really need is one taxi, so let's make do and see if we can all fit. After all, how bad could it be? I am willing to take a lap."

With the taxi packed with team members and boxes -- and every lap filled with supplies or a team member, few were certain this was really a good idea. It was very hot and dusty as the driver attempted to navigate the precarious dirt roads with the taxi shocks hitting bottom and Lolo's head frequently bouncing off the ceiling. The taxi was almost silent *and the mood quite tense* when Lolo broke into song. "Great is Thy faithfullness, Oh God our Father. Morning by morning new mercies we see. All we have needed Your hands have provided. Great is Your faithfullness unto this team."

God had obviously provided our transportation and throughout the outreach He had been so truly faithful. A chorus of voices joined in song; smiles replaced frowns and the circumstances seemed far more comical than uncomfortable. Each time a head bounced from the ceiling of that taxi, laughter followed.

After over an hour of song and laughter in the taxi, the team finally reached the village hot and tired, but surprisingly all smiles. As villagers watched so many people and supplies spill out of that single taxi, they saw love in action. The team's JOYFUL self-sacrifice spoke volumes.

On this day a small village in Africa witnessed God's love through the difficultly of delivering seed, mosquito nets, Bibles and JOY to Africa.

There was no doubt, GREAT is His Faithfullness!

Life Principle: Prayer Changes You and Your Circumstances

Life Principle: The Attitude You Choose Impacts Everything You Do

Life Principle: Being Victorious in Trials Brings Comfort and Hope to Others

Life Principle: Love Your Neighbor and You are Loving God

Life Principle: Glory in your Tribulations for They Produce Perseverance

www.ingramcontent.com/pod-product-compliance
Lightning Source LLC
Chambersburg PA
CBHW060941040426

42445CB00011B/957